OVERCOMING
FEAR

ELIMINATING THE BONDAGE OF FEAR

CREFLO DOLLAR

Overcoming Fear: Eliminating the Bondage of Fear

ISBN 978-1-64079-563-1 (hardcover)
ISBN 978-1-64079-561-7 (paperback)
ISBN 978-1-64079-562-4 (digital)
LCCN: 2017942878

Christian Faith Publishing, Inc.
296 Chestnut Street
Meadville, PA 16335
www.christianfaithpublishing.com

Printed in the United States of America

This book is dedicated to my mother, Emma Dollar, whose unwavering resilience has encouraged me to patiently persevere through all things.

CONTENTS

ACKNOWLEDGEMENT

I would like to express my gratitude to the many people who saw me through this project by providing support, encouragement, comments, and feedback.

I would like to thank my in-house editorial staff for the time you spent working on and supervising this project. Your anointing and skills are an asset to the ministry.

Thanks to my executive staff for making sure all the logistics of publishing this book were handled in a professional and timely manner.

To my partners, friends, supporters, and the entire World Changers family, I say thank you for your continuous love, support, and prayers. Together, we continue to share God's love and grace globally, making a mark that truly cannot be erased.

A special thank you to my wife, Taffi, and our children for allowing me the time to fulfill the will of God for my life. Your love and support mean everything to me.

Ultimately, I thank my heavenly Father who has made all things possible for those who believe.

INTRODUCTION

Fear is more than a figment of our imaginations or something that can be overcome merely by exercising willpower. The world would have us to believe it is a normal part of life; however, there is nothing natural or normal about fear, and it should never be tolerated on any level. In fact, I will go so far as to say that fear is a cancer that is affecting people from all walks of life. It is a spiritual force that is designed by the enemy to steal, kill, and destroy.

I remember a time when fear was a major stronghold in my life, as well as in the life of my wife, Taffi. My own personal experience with fear stemmed from a tragic death in my family that took place when I was in college. I had a female relative who went out one night and mysteriously disappeared. She was later found dead in the trunk of a car.

This experience impacted me in a tremendous way because it was through this tragedy that the enemy planted a seed of fear in my soul that surfaced when I married Taffi. The fear of something happening to her when she left the house frequently tormented me. Fear had gained a foothold in my life. I would sit home waiting for her, and when she finally walked through the door I would explode in anger. She couldn't figure out the root of my issue. Later, I finally told her what had happened to my aunt.

Years went by, and I was still never really comfortable with her going anywhere by herself, particularly when we started a church in New York. Taffi would want to catch cabs or walk around Manhattan, and I would go into panic mode every time. One day, the Lord spoke to me and said, "If you don't get rid of this fear concerning your wife's protection, you're going to be credited with any type of harm that comes to her." What a hard word! When I heard it, my immediate reaction was to defend my position by letting God know I had to take care of her, until He told me He could take care of her better than I could. He reminded me of His promise of angelic protection and how those who dwell in the secret place of the Most High are kept safe. I had to take Him at His Word, and release the fear of something happening to my wife. Only then was I able to turn over everything pertaining to my wife and kids to God. I have since learned to have peace about their safety. *God* takes care of us, which is why I don't have to stress out about it.

My story is just one of millions of similar encounters with the spirit of fear, and it is also a testament to the power of God residing in each of us to overcome it. When we get to the place where we refuse to tolerate fear in any form, it *has* to leave. And when fear leaves, Satan leaves. This book is designed to expose the spirit of fear in all its forms and show you how faith in God brings the victory. His love not only transcends the spirit of fear, but it flushes it out. By developing in the love of God and getting away from an attitude of self-preservation, we can begin to live fear-free lives, *every day*.

As you carefully digest and apply the truths revealed in this book, I pray that the spirit of fear will leave your life as well. God's covenant is full of promises that cover every possible area of fear, and through our faith, those promises can become a reality. Now, let's discover the truth about fear.

CHAPTER 1
Understanding the Laws That Govern Life

"I call heaven and earth to record this day against you, that I have set before you life and death, blessing and cursing: therefore choose life, that both thou and thy seed may live"

(Deuteronomy 30:19).

Nothing just happens. I know that goes against a lot of religious thinking and ideas about why certain things take place and who is to blame, but the truth of the matter is everything that transpires in this earth and in our lives happens for a reason. When we understand the laws that govern life, we become aware of how *our* involvement with certain spiritual principles can actually *activate* things in our lives—good or bad. Forget about being powerless against the enemy and being subject to the havoc he wants to wreak. The choices *we* make are the catalysts to God *or* Satan having access to our lives. We have the power to do something about where we are and to prevent the catastrophes that are designed to destroy our faith in God.

Everything starts with an understanding of the laws that govern life. What is a law? It is an established principle that will work for anyone who will get involved with it. The laws that govern life are those unseen spiritual principles that, when activated, will result in certain consequences. Your knowledge of these laws, and the results of turning them on, can be the difference between life and death.

If you are unfamiliar with the concept of spiritual laws and how they work, I want you to consider some natural laws that operate along the same lines and have inevitable results. For example, the law of gravity says that whatever goes up must come down. It is an undeniable, irrefutable law of nature. Simply put, there is no way any of us are getting around it. Even if you don't believe gravity works, it doesn't change the fact that if you jump off the top of a skyscraper, you are going to fall to the ground. Gravity is a law that will work every time, for *anyone* who will get involved with it. There are also laws of physics, laws that govern an object's ability to take flight, etc. Laws govern the universe in which we live.

Now, when it comes to the things that go on in our lives personally, there are also laws in operation that we must be aware of. These are spiritual laws, or principles, that will also work for anyone who will get involved. The results of activating them are as guaranteed as the law of gravity. Unfortunately, most people's ignorance of spiritual laws results in a lot of problems.

We all have to come to the point of realizing that continuing to make excuses to justify where we are is not going to change our situation. If we don't get hold of the importance of understanding the laws that govern life, we will continue to blame God and the devil when things go wrong. Now I'm not saying the devil doesn't have a hand in some of the negative things that happen, but he can only do what we grant him permission to do. Even he operates through our activation of spiritual laws. And so, we've got to get to the place where we begin to recognize that things don't just happen. They happen because there was some kind of law that was put into motion. The good news is that once you realize that you can do something about your situation, you can begin to change the course of your life.

THE TWO PRIMARY LAWS

When we talk about spiritual laws, just like natural laws, there are two that stand out as the primary principles under which many others fall. These are the Law of the Spirit of Life in Christ Jesus and the Law of Sin and Death. I like to look at these two laws as reciprocals. You probably are most familiar with the word *reciprocal* when you think about dealing with fractions. In school, we learned that a reciprocal is an inversion. For example, the reciprocal of the fraction 3/4 is 4/3. Both of them are fractions, but one is just the inverted, or opposite version of the other. Another example of a reciprocal would be points North and South on a compass. Both are directions, but they are opposites. This is also the case in the spirit realm. For everything God has created that falls under the Law of the Spirit of Life in Christ Jesus, there exists a spiritual reciprocal. The Law of the Spirit of Life in Christ Jesus and everything it encompasses is diametrically opposed to the Law of Sin and Death. Both will yield dramatically different results in your life if activated. Knowing is half the battle.

You may be wondering what the Law of the Spirit of Life in Christ Jesus encompasses. It covers everything God has promised in His Word—the blessing, eternal life, faith, a recreated human spirit, peace, prosperity, the gifts of the Spirit, healing, deliverance, protection, the Holy Spirit, the fruit of the Spirit, and more. It is the law that governs the Kingdom of God.

On the other end of the spectrum is the Law of Sin and Death, which governs Satan's kingdom, the Kingdom of Darkness. This law is the reciprocal of the Law of Life in Christ Jesus and includes fear, the curse, sin, condemnation, bondage, poverty, oppression and depression, addiction, sickness, physical death, and ultimately, separation from God in Hell. The Law of Sin and Death, when operating in your life, will result in a miserable existence both on earth and after death. It is from this law that Jesus came to redeem every man.

Now, one of the things I've recognized is that there are two opposing spiritual forces in operation. Every person will have to choose which system he or she will yield to, which will turn on either of these two laws. Faith allows God in your life while fear is an entry point through which Satan gains access. Faith falls under the category of the Law of the Spirit of Life in Christ Jesus, and fear falls under the Law of Sin and Death. Fear operates in the same way faith does—by corresponding action—but it will bring about very different results in your life.

I like to look at faith as the currency of the Kingdom of

God. It is the "substance" you need to bring to God in exchange for His promises. Faith is the substance of things hoped for, the evidence of things unseen (Hebrews 11:1). Without faith, it is impossible to please God, and it is also impossible to receive from Him. You must have faith in order to lay hold of the things the Bible promises. It is the spiritual force that turns on the Law of the Spirit of Life in Christ Jesus.

Fear, being faith's reciprocal, is the exact opposite. It is also a spiritual force, but instead of connecting you with the things of God, it connects you to Satan's plan for your life. Many people think having fear keeps them safe, when in reality it opens them up to every destructive force the enemy can unleash in their lives. It is the substance of things you don't want to happen to you, and it is the evidence that what you are afraid of will eventually manifest. Fear pleases Satan because it gives him full access into every area of your life.

The biblical story of Job is a prime example of what can happen when the Law of Fear is activated. Job was a well-known man who was extremely wealthy. He had a large family, which consisted of seven sons and three daughters. He was righteous in God's eyes and sought to please the Lord. However, the one area in which he allowed Satan access was where his family was concerned. You see, Job feared that his children would sin against the Lord, causing something bad to happen to them. As a result, he continually offered sacrifices to God on their behalf. The problem was that his actions were completely fear-based.

Believe it or not, Job's fear actually allowed the devil to

destroy his children, as well as his goods. Job 3:25 says, "*For the thing I greatly feared is come upon me, and that which I was afraid of is come unto me.*" Instead of trusting God with his children, he feared something would happen to them. As a result, he turned on a negative spiritual law. I often tell parents who constantly worry about their children that worrying is not going to do anything to protect them. In fact, worry is a form of fear; it is not noble or spiritual. Many times, when it comes to our kids, we somehow feel justified, as parents, to worry. But it is actually one of the most dangerous things we can do as far as our children's welfare is concerned. The enemy is seeking to steal, kill, and destroy our lives, and he is able to accomplish it through the avenue of fear.

WHICH LAW WILL YOU CHOOSE?

It is amazing to me that most people tend to hear Satan more clearly than they hear God. They listen to him say they're not going to make it, that they are going to fail, that they're going to be depressed, sick, and broke all their lives. However, understanding the nature of Satan will give you the strength you need to resist his deception and *choose* to activate the Law of Faith rather than the Law of Fear.

The first thing we must know about Satan is that he is a liar. He *cannot* tell the truth! Similarly, God is the truth and *cannot* tell a lie. The very natures of God and Satan are what govern the words they speak. When God says something to you, you can bank on it because He is incapable of lying. When Satan whispers something in your ear, you can be sure it is a lie because he is incapable of telling the truth. When you understand the fundamental differences between God and Satan, your confidence in your ability to rise above fear will soar.

The Bible doesn't just call Satan a liar; it says he is the *father of lies*. He has never created anything; he has only perverted what God has created. His primary goal is to challenge God's faith-giving promises with fear, which brings doubt. When we understand Satan's tactics, along with the law of reciprocals, we begin to see that every time we embrace fear of any kind, we are cancelling out our faith.

Second Peter 1:1-4 says:

> *Simon Peter, a servant and an apostle of Jesus Christ, to them that have obtained like precious faith with us through the righteousness of God and our Saviour Jesus Christ: Grace and peace be multiplied unto you through the knowledge of God, and of Jesus our Lord, According as his divine power hath given unto us all things that pertain unto life and godliness, through the knowledge of him that hath called us to glory and virtue: Whereby are given unto us exceeding great and precious promises: that by these ye might be partakers of the divine nature, having escaped the corruption that is in the world through lust.*

This passage of Scripture says that God has given us *all* things that pertain to life and godliness. This means there is a promise that covers every single area and situation in your life. The problem comes when you don't know there is a promise of God that covers your circumstance and situation. When you are unaware of God's promises, you will yield to the Law of Fear, and it will begin to dominate you. And when fear dominates your life, faith is quenched.

The powerful thing about God's Word is that when you locate a promise of God, you locate the faith it takes to bring it to pass. From the start, you have already been given the advantage where your faith is concerned. Every scripture has faith built into it, which, when deposited in your heart, will pull the unseen spiritual things into the natural realm. However, you cannot allow your faith to be short-circuited by giving in to fear.

Remember, the enemy's primary goal is to get you to doubt that God's Word will come to pass in your life. In other words, every fear that will ever confront you in life, no matter what that fear is, is designed to nullify the promises God has made to you. For example, a fear of getting a disease is actually a fear that is confronting the Word's declaration that by the stripes of Jesus you have been healed (1 Peter 2:24). The fear that someone is going to rob you, break into your home, or hurt you is a fear that is confronting God's promise of divine protection for those who are in covenant with Him (Psalm 91). Every fear you face opposes the faith and promises of God.

When you know the purpose of Satan's attacks, and you know his lying nature, you are positioned to ward off his attacks. Anything he says should never be internalized. In fact, when he threatens you through fear, it should be your indication that the exact opposite is true! Ultimately, it becomes a matter of making up your mind to believe God's Word instead of giving in to fear.

God has given every person free will, meaning we all have the ability to make our own decisions. Fear is indeed a spiritual force, but it has no power except what you give it. You can choose a better way—the Law of Faith—which activates the salvation God wants us all to have and experience.

One of our ministry partners shared a testimony with me about how God preserved him in the midst of a dangerous situation because he had faith in God's divine protection rather than fear of being harmed. The individual had gone camping with his family. One night they were at the campsite fellowshipping and reading their Bibles, and before settling in for the evening, they prayed to the Lord to watch over them, and they released the angels of God to protect them.

Later on that night, a motorcycle gang invaded the camp site and began to harass

> "WHEN YOU CHOOSE TO YIELD TO THE LAW OF FEAR, YOU ARE ESSENTIALLY SUBMITTING YOURSELF TO THE LAW OF SIN AND DEATH."

them. All of a sudden, the bikers jumped on their motorcycles and just took off. After the gang had left, the man and his family gathered around the fire and started praising and thanking God for the victory.

What they didn't know was that someone in the group had a camera that had dropped on the ground and happened to snap a picture of the scene. It wasn't until later, when he got home and developed the roll of film that he discovered the photograph that was snapped by the camera was a picture of an angel! God's divine protection had manifested in the midst of a dangerous situation because of this family's decision to choose faith in God's Word over fear.

When you choose to yield to the Law of Fear, you are essentially submitting yourself to the Law of Sin and Death. Like Job discovered, fear opens the door to the destructive power of Satan. But everything begins with a choice. Deuteronomy 30:19 says, "*I call heaven and earth to record this day against you, that I have set before you life and death, blessing and cursing: therefore choose life, that both thou and thy seed may live.*" Death is the reciprocal of life, blessing is the reciprocal of cursing, and God says, "*If you don't know what to choose, I'll give you a hint—choose life.*" Faith is a life choice, and when you don't choose faith, you are choosing fear by default, and it *will* begin to operate in your life.

Please understand that a decision is not something that randomly happens in your mind. A decision is confirmed by what you allow to pass before your eyes, what you let go through your ears, what you speak out of your mouth, and ultimately what you plant in your heart. It is only through corresponding action that you know you have made a decision for or against something.

A lot of people think that belief is just a passive activity that happens inside of them. No, belief is *action*. When you act in a way that demonstrates your faith, even through the words you speak, you are choosing faith over fear. You can't really say you've made the decision to choose faith if you still give your attention to the bad news reported on television, which will cause you to speak words that are full of fear, doubt, and unbelief. You can't subscribe to the world's way of thinking and expect to have faith.

If you want the things of God to work, it's going to require you to turn on the Law of Faith by filling your spirit with the Word of God and speaking it out of your mouth. Saturating yourself with God's promises will deposit all the faith "dynamite" you need in your heart so you can absolutely override the Law of Fear. Meditate on the Word, keep it before your eyes, and listen to it regularly. Confess it every day, multiple times a day, and allow it to become your final authority. The laws that govern life are so easy to activate, which is why you want to be sure you are activating the right ones.

You can make the decision today to break out of the fear-filled life. Contrary to what the world may say, fear is not beneficial in any way. Whatever bondage you or a loved one may be experiencing can actually be traced back to fear. The good news is that if it is present, the Law of the Spirit of Life in Christ Jesus has the power to annihilate it. Allow the faith of God to drive the fear, doubt, and unbelief out of your life. Activate positive spiritual laws so you can live the life God intends for you to have. The choice is yours!

CHAPTER 2
Set Free from Bondage

*"For ye have not received the spirit of
bondage again to fear; but ye have received
the Spirit of adoption, whereby we cry,
Abba, Father"*

(Romans 8:15).

Is it possible to jump in a lake or an ocean and not get wet? The obvious answer is no; it is not possible to come in contact with water and not get wet—the two are a package deal! When it comes to something we can tangibly perceive, like water and our senses, it tends to be easier to accept the fact that being wet comes with the water. However, when it comes to intangible spiritual forces, like fear and faith, sometimes it takes us a little longer to process the connection between spiritual laws and the reason why certain things happen. Just like water causes us to get wet when we come in contact with it, fear brings torment into our lives when we give place to it. It is an inevitable result of allowing fear to dominate your thinking. Fear is a dangerous spiritual force that is synonymous with bondage.

When we begin to understand and apply spiritual laws and principles, it becomes clear that fear is something that cannot be tolerated in any way, shape, or form in our lives. God needs our faith in order to manifest His promises in our lives. On the other hand, Satan needs fear to operate in our lives.

There is no denying that we live in a fear-filled world, where being afraid is the norm. Most people have one or more nagging fears that affect their thinking on a daily basis and impact them in ways they do not even realize. In addition, the media seems to be committed to pumping fear into the minds of the general public through their negative reports. If we give attention to what is going on in the world more than we do the Word of God, we can easily become victims of fear and its negative consequences.

There are several scriptures that bear witness to the truth about fear and what comes with it. Romans 8:15 says, "For ye have not received the spirit of bondage again to fear; but ye have received the Spirit of adoption, whereby we cry, Abba, Father." According to this scripture, there are a few things to note about fear. First, it is something that has to be received from the outside, which means it is not a characteristic of our re-born spirits. It also brings with it a spirit of bondage. Second Timothy 1:7 says that God does not give us the spirit of fear, but that He gives us power, love, and a sound mind with which we are to govern our lives. Clearly, fear is a foreign spirit that comes from the enemy of our souls, not God. It is something we have to *receive* from the outside in.

What does it mean to be in bondage? *Webster's Dictionary* defines bondage as "the condition of being involuntarily subject to a power, force, or influence." This is exactly what happens when we yield to fear. Hebrews 2:15 also says, *"And delivers them who through fear of death were all their lifetime subject to bondage."* People get in bondage to all kinds of things that stem from fear. Whether it is the fear of people's opinions or the fear of flying, fear is designed to attack people's minds and subject them to the negative power of the devil. It is important to remember that *any* kind of fear, regardless of how insignificant you think it is, will put you in bondage.

DEALING WITH THE SIN OF FEAR

Most people do not consider being in fear a sin, but according to the Bible, God classifies it as such. That may be a hard pill to swallow, but knowing the truth about fear will only equip you to resist it. Romans 14:23 says, *"And he that doubteth is damned if he eat, because he eateth not of faith: for whatsoever is not of faith is sin."* What an awesome statement. God is saying that if we are walking in fear, we are walking in sin. Why? It is because fear is rebellion against God and His way of doing things. God honors faith because it demonstrates your trust in Him. It is the master key to getting things to work in your life. But when you operate in fear, you are giving Satan exactly what he wants. And giving Satan what he wants causes us to sin against God. Make no mistake about it, fear is supported by a demonic spirit that will absolutely destroy your life.

Revelation 21:8 puts fear in a very distinct category, one that is on the same level as murder, sexual sin, witchcraft, and lying. It says that people who do these things, including those who walk in fear, have their part in the lake that burns with fire and brimstone. Thank God for the blood of Jesus and His wonderful grace that saved us from this judgement of sin.

I want to examine this issue of bondage as it relates to the spirit of fear. We understand that whenever we walk in fear, we put ourselves in bondage to the things we are afraid of, and they can literally begin to control us. In addition to becoming a slave to the things we fear, we invite harassment and torment into our lives. This is the pressure that comes to try to keep us in a constant state of fear. It is the voice of the enemy that says, "You're going to die. You'll never make it. You'll be broke for the rest of your life." Oppression and torment are designed to have us continually acting on and receiving fear.

Jesus experienced this very harassment when the enemy came to tempt Him in the wilderness. Matthew 4:1-11 gives the account of Jesus' temptation and documents how persistent the enemy was in trying to get Him to receive words of fear. I can only imagine the discipline it took for Jesus to rise above His flesh and resist the thoughts and suggestions of the devil. Jesus stood strong until the end and refused to succumb to fear of any kind. He reminded Satan of what was written in the Word of God and forced the enemy to leave Him. As a result, the power of God showed up and put a stop to the harassment.

You and I have the same ability that Jesus did to resist fear when it shows up. Satan is not a gentleman; he will do everything he can to force his way into our consciousness by speaking his fear-filled lies to our hearts and minds so he can torment and harass us. It is up to us to allow the power of God to come on the scene and put a stop to it. We do this by *refusing* to accept fear when it knocks on our door.

DON'T ACCEPT THE TORMENT

Sometimes it amazes me how we put up with different things in our immediate world, but when it comes to the harassment of the devil, we sit idly by while he takes us for a ride. For example, sexual harassment in the workplace is not tolerated, and neither would most people tolerate someone threatening to harm their family or loved ones. If you have ever been in either of these situations, you know how quick you were to speak out and take action against such behavior from others. But somehow, we tend to be less aggressive and less proactive when Satan brings fear to our doorstep. That has got to change. Like Jesus, we must open our mouths and declare what is written in the Word of God.

As Christians, we are in a battle; it is a battle for our minds. Satan knows that if he can infiltrate a person's mind with fear, he can control his or her life. However, Isaiah 54:14 makes a promise to those who are a part of God's family, *"In righteousness shalt thou be established: thou shalt be far from oppression; for thou shalt not fear: and from terror; for it shall not come near thee."*

This scripture is God's answer for every Believer who has ever battled fear of any kind. It is a promise from heaven. We don't have to sit back and put up with the harassment of terror and fear. When we choose not to receive it, the Bible says it won't come near us.

This is a revelation that we must get a hold of and begin to imprint on our conscious minds. We do *not* have to be subject to fear. The choice is entirely up to us. While fear and terror may be on the rise in the world, and may even try to come against us, they are powerless against the person who has confidence in God's Word and keeps it at the forefront of his or her thinking at all times.

Whatever you give your attention to is what will become large in your life. If you allow fear to dominate your thinking by giving attention to your fears, those things will actually increase in your mind and heart. If you never counteract those negative thoughts and feelings with the Word of God, they will begin to frame the way you see things and ultimately begin attracting the very things you are afraid of. They will keep you in bondage, and torment you day and night. Fear is an absolute disruption of the peace God desires us to experience as Christians. We have to make a decision to keep our minds focused on what God says at all times.

> "WE DON'T HAVE TO SIT BACK AND PUT UP WITH THE HARASSMENT OF TERROR AND FEAR."

I can recall a situation that the enemy used against Taffi and me in an attempt to inject fear in our lives. There was a woman who began writing to the ministry, declaring that she and I were involved in an adulterous affair. She continued making false statements, and it was becoming very aggravating. We decided the best course of action was to pray for the woman rather than to address her. Taffi didn't allow fear or doubt to enter her mind concerning the situation because she refused to give any attention to it. Instead, she kept her focus on God's Word and His will for our lives. When it comes to the enemy's attacks of fear, the best thing you can do is ignore him and continue to focus on the Word.

A fear-filled mind will believe the lies of the enemy. When people try to put fear in you through their actions or words, show Satan you mean business by refusing to move from your stance on the Word of God.

WATCH YOUR WORDS

When it comes to fear, our words play a critical role in accepting the torment that comes with fear. The tongue is the ignition switch that activates the forces of darkness in our lives. Proverbs 18:21 says, "*Death and life are in the power of the tongue: and they that love it shall eat the fruit thereof.*" That is a powerful statement because it makes it absolutely clear that we are responsible for turning on spiritual laws. We are the establishing witnesses who determine whether fear has an opportunity to gain access into our minds.

Satan wants to get us to doubt God's ability and willingness to provide for our needs. When we speak words of doubt and unbelief, we agree with the fear. For instance, by saying things like, "I'm never going to get out of this situation" or "It seems like I'm never going to be healed from this illness," we are, in essence, "taking" the fear that is attached to those words. Once we give voice to negative thoughts, we set the corresponding spiritual law in motion. Words are powerful activators.

The worst thing you can do in a pressure situation, where fear-filled emotions are trying to overwhelm you, is to speak negatively and agree with the fear you feel on the inside. I learned about this when I was going through a period of depression and was unsure how to handle it.

Depression is anger turned inward, and it is an attack of the enemy. As I was going through this tormenting time, I had to make up my mind to resist the devil with everything I had. I became desperate and was willing to do whatever I had to do to overcome the negative emotions I was feeling.

I learned that fear simply cannot stop grace. One day I was praying and I heard the Lord say, "I want you to put the Word on your mouth four times a day." I knew what I had to do. As I began to confess the Scriptures over and over again, I was hearing myself speak the Word of God. As a result of hearing it, it was going in my heart. I had stumbled across a spiritual law and didn't even realize it! I was constantly keeping the Word before my eyes, speaking it out of my mouth, and pouring it in my ears, which was life to my spirit. I had activated the Law of the Spirit of Life in Christ Jesus, and it began to push the fear out of my heart and mind. Before long, I began to sense the joy of the Lord rising and the strength of God returning to my life.

Whether you are battling depression, doubt, insecurity, or some other fear-related issue, the key to overcoming it is to take God's Word, which imparts faith and drives out fear, and refuse to take the fear of the enemy. The life of God's Word will cast death and fear out every time, so it is vital that you continually put the Word in your mouth and make a habit of confessing it. God's grace will help you every step of the way.

KEYS TO BREAKING OUT OF TORMENT

The strategy of torment is designed to move you into acting on fear and to give Satan the ability to move in your life. How do you deal with it? Let me give you three ways:

1. **Speak against torment.**

   Don't sit there and allow tormenting thoughts to minister to you. You *must* open your mouth and speak against torment. When the devil says you're not going to make it or that you're going to die, don't sit there and keep your mouth closed. Declare the Word of God with boldness, and in faith. Find the scriptures that deal with your particular situation and fire them at Satan with intensity.

2. **Act against torment.**

   Now we know we have to get our mouths involved with the process, but there is another piece involved. You have to do something that sends a clear message to Satan that you are not succumbing to the fear he's trying to put on you. For example, if you have a tormenting fear of flying in an airplane, first find scriptures that deal with divine protection and the ministry of angels, and second, get on an airplane and fly to your next out-of-town destination. If you have a fear of heights, find the tallest building in your city and take an elevator ride all the way to the top! You may get queasy or feel ill, but at least you will be on your way to becoming free from the torment. To tell you the truth, your freedom from torment is a part of the finished works of Jesus. Be free!

3. **Continue to consistently speak and act against torment.**

Consistency is the key to the breakthrough. You cannot expect to experience sustained victory over fear if you don't make speaking and acting against it a way of life. This simply means that *every* time fear shows up to intimidate you, you immediately counterattack it. Not only that, but it also means regularly seeking out things you can do to overcome the fear. As you act against torment on purpose, and in faith, the Holy Spirit will back you up, and Satan will have no choice but to retreat.

GUARD YOUR MIND

Proverbs 4:23 says, "*Keep thy heart with all diligence; for out of it are the issues of life.*" The heart of a man is his spirit, and attached to the spirit is the soul, which includes the mind, will, and emotions. The Word tells us to guard our hearts. We do this by being good custodians over our thought lives. What we meditate on in abundance will eventually overtake and overwhelm our lives. If harassment from Satan comes and we don't develop a vigilant stance over our minds, he will continue to inject more and more negative thoughts. Before long, he will have enough "material" to build a stronghold, and you will find yourself operating in a fear that you didn't even realize was present.

We must choose what we will meditate on and what we will allow into our hearts by diligently screening what is being introduced to our minds through words and images. When you recognize a fearful thought, capture it with the Word by saying what God says about that situation. Second Corinthians 10:5 instructs the Believer to cast down imaginations and *every* high thing that exalts itself against the knowledge of God and bring them into *captivity* to the obedience of Christ. Thoughts of death or unfavorable circumstances happening to you are contradictions to the Word and must be apprehended by speaking the right words at the moment of the mental attack. When I discovered that I could capture negative thoughts, I began to bombard the spirit realm with the spoken Word of God until my mind was transformed.

If you are presently being oppressed by the torment of fear, have confidence and faith in the fact that Jesus' mission was to set you free from the harassment of the enemy. Acts 10:38 says that Jesus went about doing good and healing all those who were harassed and oppressed by the devil, for God was with Him. For every person who is being tormented by fear, Jesus has the cure—grace, which produces the burden-removing, yoke-destroying power of God. The anointing of God will put a stop to *all* forms of fear and will absolutely eradicate the torment that comes with it. All you have to do is receive the promise by faith and begin speaking and acting on it. Capture negative thoughts by declaring the Word of God. You have been set free from the bondage of fear so walk in your freedom!

CHAPTER 3
Redeemed from Destruction

"Who redeemeth thy life from destruction..."
(Psalm 103:4).

I'm sure you can remember what you were doing when you heard the news of the World Trade Center being attacked by terrorists on September 11, 2001. I remember the day before the attack happened, and how I didn't get any sleep that night because my spirit was so restless. Throughout the night, I kept saying, "*Something is wrong. Something is getting ready to happen. What in the world is going on?*" I couldn't put my finger on what was troubling me, but the next morning it became evident that the Holy Spirit had been dealing with me about something so significant that it would rock this very nation to its core.

The next morning the shocking news was being broadcast from every available news media outlet; terrorists had hijacked two U.S. airplanes and, with calculated planning, crashed both of them into each tower at the World Trade Center in lower Manhattan. In addition, a third terrorist ambushed airplane was flown into the Pentagon in Washington D.C., and another hijacked plane was in the process of being used as a murderous weapon of mass destruction.

These horrific attacks were the result of some demon-possessed individuals who decided they would be doing God a favor by coming against the United States and hitting the country where it would hurt the most—New York City, the financial epicenter of the nation. From a spiritual perspective, these heinous acts were Satan's attempt to put fear in the hearts of the American people.

Can you imagine being in one of those airplanes and knowing that you were about to die? There were accounts of many victims calling their loved ones to say goodbye. Many lives were lost, yet there were those who survived and lived to tell their stories. In the midst of it all, one of the most common questions I have heard people ask is, *"How could God let something like this happen?"* How could a loving God allow such massive destruction to take place?

I began to think about those people who had loved-ones who died in the attack and some of the questions that may have gone through their minds. I am sure there are those who began to doubt God or question if there even is a God. Others who experienced His life-saving hand in the midst of the carnage were only strengthened in their faith through the tragedy. And yet, we must make sure that we properly discern the Word of God and understand the truth about why bad things happen, what we can do to prevent certain things from taking place, and more importantly, the promise of divine protection that is found in the Bible. Our lives have been redeemed from destruction.

WE HAVE AN ENEMY

When it comes to the question, "Why do bad things happen?" the answer is simple: we have an enemy, and his name is Satan. As much as popular culture would like to downplay the reality that there is an actual evil spiritual being at work on the earth, the Word of God is true. Satan is a fallen angel whom the Bible refers to as "the god of this world" (2 Corinthians 4:4). This simply means that he is the ruling force of this current world system. He hates mankind, and his objective is to steal, kill, and destroy (John 10:10). He uses fear as a tactic to accomplish his purposes. In the case of the 9/11 attacks, his tool was terrorism, which is the organized use of fear. When we accept the fear and internalize it, we hand over our power to Satan. He needs us to be afraid in order for him to be successful in his maneuvers against us.

Knowing we have an enemy who embodies evil and wants to destroy us gives us some insight into exactly why bad things happen. One thing is for sure; God is not responsible for killing innocent people and causing devastation to communities. As long as life, as we know it, exists on the planet, our adversary will stop at nothing to cause as much deliberate pain and death as he can. And, he is banking on Christians not knowing their authority as Believers, or the

> "AS CHILDREN OF GOD, WE ARE IN A PLACE OF ABSOLUTE AUTHORITY OVER SATAN."

power of God's Word, in order to carry out his destructive plans.

UNDERSTANDING OUR POSITION

When we understand that we have an enemy who is at war with mankind, it becomes clear that as Believers we are involved in a spiritual battle of epic proportions. If you follow Jesus Christ, Satan particularly hates you because you are responsible for shedding light on his tactics as well as sharing the Gospel of Jesus Christ with others. Satan is opposed to anything having to do with God, and he wants us to remain ignorant of the authority we possess through our relationship with Jesus. We must understand our spiritual position in Christ in order to shield ourselves from the enemy's attacks.

Knowing what it means to be "saved" gives us a new perspective on dealing with fear and any attack of the enemy to try to harm us. Before coming to the knowledge of Jesus Christ, all of us were in sin. In fact, the only prerequisite to being a sinner is to be born. The Word says we were all "shaped in iniquity" (Psalm 51:5) in our mothers' wombs. While growing up, unless we were taught the things of God at a young age, we adopted mindsets and behaviors that went against the Bible. This is simply the result of being born into this current world system which is governed by fear, sickness, disease, spiritual oppression, and death. Unless we make a decision for Christ and renew our minds, we are subject to everything the enemy has planned for us, and his ultimate goal is to destroy our lives.

On the other side of the spectrum is a Kingdom and way of operating that ensures life, peace, health, protection, joy, success, and prosperity in life—the Kingdom of God. When we accept Jesus as our Lord and Savior, we are instantly moved out of the jurisdiction of Satan's world system and into the light of God's Kingdom. In essence, we no longer belong to the devil, which means he has no legal right to have access to us. This is not to say there will not be struggles, tests, trials, and temptations that we go through when he attempts to get us off track; however, when we know and understand our victory in Christ, we can defeat him every time.

To be born again means to be re-created in your spirit through the power of God's love. When we accept Jesus into our hearts by faith, we are transformed on a spiritual level, and we are given certain "benefits." One of the benefits of the salvation package is divine protection and redemption from death, both spiritual and physical. It is up to us, however, to get in the Word of God and find out exactly how to appropriate these wonderful promises from the Father. What you don't know *can* hurt you, which is why it is imperative that we discover everything we can about this vital subject.

As children of God, we are in a place of absolute authority over Satan. This is a powerful truth that will revolutionize the way we interact with life on a daily basis. Our position is one of power and it is through our relationship with Jesus Christ that we are able to claim this spiritual status. Ephesians 2:4-6 says, *"But God, who is rich in mercy, for his great love wherewith he loved* us, *Even when we were dead in sins, hath quickened us together with Christ, (by grace ye are saved;) And hath raised us up together, and made us sit together in heavenly places in Christ Jesus."*

We see in this scripture that while we may inhabit the earthly realm as human beings, from a spiritual, standpoint we are actually seated with Christ in heavenly places, *far* above every demonic spirit that exists (Ephesians 1:21). What an empowering truth! If fear, death, destruction, and mayhem are spiritual forces that are activated by wicked spirits, then according to the Word of God we are in a much *higher* spiritual position. Why then, would we even entertain fear of what the devil can do to us? It is our awareness of just how powerful God is that enables us to be victorious over the devil.

REDEEMED FROM DEATH

Did you know there are people who go through life afraid that something bad will happen to them at every turn? They are completely controlled by the spirit of fear, and, as we have discovered, fear will connect you to the very things you are afraid of. One fear that plagues so many individuals is the fear of death. People are afraid of dying because they are really unsure about what is on the other side of life. Facing death without the knowledge of Jesus Christ is a scary thought. And yet, I often think about the many people trapped in the Twin Towers on September 11 and wonder how many of them knew the Lord as they faced an uncertain future. However, for those who had a personal relationship with the Lord, their futures were secure. Even though they may have perished in the tragic disaster, they were on their way to heaven.

I have often said that on September 11, there were three groups of people who had very significant experiences at the World Trade Center that day. First, there were those who heard the voice of God and obeyed what they heard. Second, there were those who heard the voice of God and chose not to obey what they heard. And finally, there were those who couldn't recognize the voice of God at all. Each individual in each of these three categories experienced different things that fateful day. Likewise, in our lives, where we are in regards to these three categories can be the difference between deliverance and disaster.

The Bible says that the steps of a righteous man are ordered by God. It also says that our lives are redeemed from destruction (Psalm 103:1-7). We know that God cannot lie and that He always performs His Word (Jeremiah 1:12). This simply means that if God says it, it is the conclusion of the matter. If He says our lives are redeemed from destruction, it then becomes our responsibility to believe and receive the promise by faith. This is the first thing we must do to activate our deliverance from the enemy's hand.

What does it mean to be righteous? It means to be in right-standing with God. We are in right-standing with God through the blood of Jesus and acknowledging God in all our ways. When we have a personal relationship with the Father through His Son, Jesus, the Word declares us righteous, and God says He will "order our steps."

Sometimes we don't even realize that our steps are being ordered, but when we are children of God, He is constantly directing, leading, and guiding us away from trouble. When you wake up every morning and declare, "My life has been redeemed from destruction," God can't help but to get involved in your daily affairs in order to keep you out of harm's way. On September 11, there were accounts of people who overslept for work for the first time in years, and even those who took an extra few minutes getting to work that day. These seemingly minor details ended up saving their lives. It is often these small decisions we make that classify our steps as being "ordered by the Lord" and can end up protecting us from danger.

Another aspect of activating the promise of redemption from destruction is that we must cultivate a relationship with God so that we can know and recognize His voice when He speaks to us. It is one thing to be unaware of the guiding hand of God, and be rescued by what seems like a simple decision to take another route to work or stay home for the day, but God wants us to get to the point where we can actually hear Him give us specific directions that are designed for our protection from all kinds of dangerous or compromising situations. It all begins with the written Word of God.

By studying and meditating on the Word, we familiarize ourselves with the voice of God. Anything He says to us will line up with the written Word and will guide us on the path to the fulfilled promise of divine protection. We actually fine-tune our spiritual hearing the more we study the Word, which makes it easier to distinguish His voice when He speaks.

Make no mistake about it; God doesn't want to speak to us in vague impressions. Most of the time, the spiritual "frequency" we are operating on determines the clarity of the message we receive from the Lord and the specificity of the instructions. Spending significant time in prayer and fellowship with God through His written Word, positions us to hear from Him in the most critical moments.

Psalm 91 contains probably some of the most well known passages of Scripture dealing with divine protection, safety, and redemption from destruction. Committing these reassuring scriptures to memory, as well as hiding them deep in our hearts, will boost our confidence in the promise of protection from all kinds of negative situations including:

1. Secret traps and deadly diseases (Psalm 91:3). Satan has numerous traps set for us on a daily basis. He also wants to destroy our lives through disease, which is on the rise today. The good news is that we are redeemed from both of these disasters when we trust God and take refuge in His presence.

2. Dangers at night (Psalm 91:5). I remember a time when my wife, Taffi, would turn all the lights on in the house when she was home alone at night, because of fear. But the Word says that God will protect us from the enemy's attacks at night. He will also protect us from the "arrows" of the enemy that fly during the daytime. Take authority over any accidents and dangerous situations that take place at night. God is faithful to protect you.

3. Destruction all around you (Psalm 91:7). We live in a dangerous world that will only get worse as demonic activity continues to increase. In the days and years ahead, we can expect to see all kinds of disasters (natural and man-made) taking place. However, we can take solace in the promises of God. He says that even though these things may be happening all around us, we will only observe them with our eyes. The wicked will fall, but we will not be touched or affected by what is going on around us.

4. Attacks against us in our homes (Psalm 91:10). There is a promise of protection for God's people and their homes. This scripture declares that no terrible disasters will strike you or your home. This includes your family and your possessions. As a child of God, you have a right to the divine protection the blood of Jesus affords. Plead the blood over your family, loved ones, possessions, and home. Take authority over home invasions, robberies, thefts, and any other attempt of the enemy to attack you in this area. Believe you receive the protection of God!

How does God carry out this promise of redemption from destruction? Through His angels! These heavenly beings are God's Covenant Enforcing Agents and are responsible for carrying out the decrees of God's Word in the lives of His people. Psalm 91:11, 12 paints a powerful portrait of angels and their divine assignments to Christians when it says, *"For he shall give his angels charge over thee, to keep thee in all thy ways. They shall bear thee up in their hands, lest thou dash thy foot against a stone."*

When you realize that you have invisible spiritual agents working on your behalf, it eradicates fear on so many levels. Angels are surrounding and guarding your home and upholding every airplane on which you are traveling. They are accompanying you wherever you go! Armed with this revelation, you should fear nothing.

GET YOUR MOUTH INVOLVED

You may have wondered why bad things happen to Christian people who believe in God. It almost seems incomprehensible how Bible-toting Believers could be the victims of crime perpetrated against them or some other disaster that claims lives. I don't have all the answers, but I do know the Word of God is true. It says our lives are redeemed from destruction. So how does the promise translate into becoming a reality in our lives on a consistent basis? The answer is simple; we must use our mouths to activate the Word of God and make it functional in our lives.

There are so many scriptures in the Bible that talk about the power of the tongue, and when it comes to divine protection, we know that angels play a major role in carrying that out. But we must speak the Word of God concerning our redemption in order for it to become a reality in our lives. It is not enough to just come to church and hear the Word preached. While this provides us with the information and revelation we need to live the Christian life, we must become proactive in appropriating what God has promised.

Psalm 107:2 says, *"Let the redeemed of the Lord say so, whom he hath redeemed from the hand of the enemy."* God clearly instructs us to *declare* our redemption. And Psalm 103:20 says the angels hearken to the *voice* of God's Word. This simply means that in order for the angels to respond, someone has to say something! If we keep our mouths shut and don't speak the Word aloud, the knowledge we have from the Word won't be effective. We must put the Word in our mouths and give God control of our situations. The enemy is rendered powerless against Believers who constantly speaks God's Word in faith and are able to hear the voice of the Lord giving them specific instructions.

Jesus says in John 14:1 (*The Amplified Bible*), *"Do not let your hearts be troubled (distressed, agitated). You believe in and adhere to and trust in and rely on God; believe in and adhere to and trust in and rely also on Me."* This encouraging Word from the Lord is not just to be applied during times of ease and tranquility, but it is something we must remember when bad things seem to be happening all around us. All over the world, events of devastating magnitude are taking place. However, we cannot allow fear to govern our lives. We have been given power, love, and a sound mind instead of the spirit of fear. When we know our rights as Believers, and put absolute faith and trust in God, we can live a peaceful, fearless life in the midst of a dangerous world. Our lives have been redeemed from destruction. Believe it, receive it, and speak it; God is faithful and will fulfill His promises!

CHAPTER 4
Destroying Fear through Covenant Awareness

"Know ye therefore that they which are of faith, the same are the children of Abraham. And the scripture, foreseeing that God would justify the heathen through faith, preached before the gospel unto Abraham, saying, In thee shall all nations be blessed. So then they which are of faith are blessed with faithful Abraham"
(Galatians 3:7-9).

Would you doubt or question your mother's or father's ability or willingness to do something they promise if they have a consistent habit of doing what they say they will do? I know I wouldn't. When you have a parent or friend whose word is their bond, and who always follows through on their promises to the best of their ability, you don't question their integrity. Now, we know that, as human beings, we can and will miss the mark; even the most faithful person can still falter. However, when you have joined God's family of Believers, you enter into a binding agreement called a covenant. It is through this covenant relationship that God's promises become real to us. Fear has no place in our lives because of our covenant with our heavenly Father. We must develop a covenant-awareness so that our faith in God is unshakable. A covenant mind-set will destroy fear.

Covenant is the foundation of everything God does. He is a covenant-making and covenant-*keeping* God. This is the platform from which our faith springs. A covenant is not the same as a contract. It is a binding agreement entered into by two or more parties who agree to carry out the terms of the covenant. In ancient times, covenants were honored to such a point that the individuals involved could only get out of the agreement through death.

Today's society doesn't have a real respect for covenants, which is why there are so many divorces and broken relationships. However, God still takes the covenant as seriously as He did thousands of years ago. We must renew our minds to what it means to be in covenant with God so we can live fear-free lives.

OUR COVENANT WITH GOD:
HOW IT ALL STARTED

In order to understand the covenant God has made with us, we need to journey back to the Garden of Eden and look at why and how the whole thing got started. You are probably familiar with the biblical account of Adam and Eve and the fall of man. In the beginning, God created mankind and gave him dominion over everything on the planet. He placed them in the Garden of Eden and gave them everything they would ever need or desire. In fact, they had no awareness of needs or wants because everything was provided for them. They were spiritually connected to the Father and had constant fellowship with Him. They lived in a type of earthly paradise because of the Blessing that was on their lives, free from lack, sickness, disease, and fear. Can you imagine what that must have been like?

Unfortunately, Adam and Eve forfeited everything that was rightfully theirs when they disobeyed God in the Garden (Genesis 3). He had given them specific directives regarding the trees from which they could eat and the one to avoid, specifically the Tree of the Knowledge of Good and Evil. But when Satan entered the Garden and began to speak words to Eve that contradicted what God had said, they took the bait. One act of selfishness ended up costing them everything. As a result, sin entered the earth, they lost their position of authority and dominion, and were connected to the curse. This was essentially the "birthplace" of fear.

From that day forward, everything became corrupted by the spirit of fear. Satan became the "god of this world" and had the legal right, because of Adam's treacherous act, to torment mankind with fear, oppression, sickness, poverty, and lack. These things were never in God's plan for mankind. Through Adam's sin, we all became natural-born sinners who were shaped in iniquity in our mother's wombs (Psalm 51:5).

Fortunately, God already had a plan in place to redeem mankind from a life of turmoil, both physically and spiritually. Jesus was the answer! However, He had to come into the earth in the form of a man, and in order for that to happen, God had to make a covenant *with* a man who would begin the process of carrying the lineage of Jesus so He could be born. This is where the covenant came into play.

The Word of God talks about how God cut a covenant with a man called Abram (whose name He would later change to Abraham). In Genesis Chapter 12, the process begins with God calling Abram to leave all that is familiar to him and journey to a land to which God sends him. The Lord promised to bless Abram and increase him to the point where a great nation would come out of him—the nation of Israel through which Jesus would be born, as well as the nation of Gentiles who would become a part of God's family through their connection to Jesus Christ. God promised that the "seed" that came out of Abraham would be more numerous than the stars in the sky (Genesis 15:5).

In Chapter 15:1-6 of Genesis, God appeared to Abram in a vision and reiterated the promise, "*After these things the word of the Lord came unto Abram in a vision, saying, Fear not, Abram: I am thy shield, and thy exceeding great reward...And he believed in the Lord; and he counted it to him for righteousness.*" God spoke faith-filled words to Abram to calm his fears and reassure him of their agreement. Abram's faith in those words connected him to the manifestation of them. There is something about God's Word that absolutely destroys fear when we grab hold of it.

The actual cutting of the covenant took place in Genesis 15:8-18. It involved blood, which is a vital part of the process. God sealed the deal with this man by walking through the blood of animals so that the experience and reality of it would be etched in Abraham's mind forever:

> And he said, Lord GOD, whereby shall I know that I shall inherit it? And he said unto him, Take me an heifer of three years old, and a she goat of three years old, and a ram of three years old, and a turtledove, and a young pigeon. And he took unto him all these, and divided them in the midst, and laid each piece one against another: but the birds divided he not. And when the fowls came down upon the carcasses, Abram drove them away. And when the sun was going down, a deep sleep fell upon Abram; and, lo, an horror of great darkness fell upon him...And it came to pass, that, when the sun went down, and it was dark, behold a smoking furnace, and a burning lamp that passed between those pieces. In the same day the LORD made a covenant with Abram, saying, Unto thy seed have I given this land, from the river of Egypt unto the great river, the river Euphrates.

Because he was a man who was probably familiar with covenant practices, God knew that this supernatural agreement would become more real to Abraham than anything he had ever known. The day God entered into covenant with Abraham was the day the redemption of mankind and the restoration of the blessing were activated.

WHERE WE FIT IN

Because fear is a part of the curse, and the curse has been taken care of by the covenant of Abraham, it is important for us to know where we fit into things. First, our relationship with Jesus Christ, by faith, is what connects us to the blessings of the covenant of Abraham. Galatians 3:7-9 says:

> Know ye therefore that they which are of faith, the same are the children of Abraham. And the scripture, foreseeing that God would justify the heathen through faith, preached before the gospel unto Abraham, saying, In thee shall all nations be blessed. So then they which are of faith are blessed with faithful Abraham."

This scripture lets us know that when we believe on God like Abraham did, we become blessed just like him. We become part of his spiritual lineage! In the same chapter, the Apostle Paul says, "Christ hath redeemed us from the curse of the law, being made a curse for us: for it is written, Cursed is every one that hangeth on a tree: That the blessing of Abraham might come on the Gentiles through Jesus Christ; that we might receive the promise of the Spirit through faith" (v. 13, 14).

Jesus literally became a curse when He was killed on the cross, which means he took upon Himself everything that was a part of the curse, including fear. When we accept Him into our hearts as our Lord and personal Savior, we receive the Blessing of God, which is the key benefit of the covenant of Abraham. Everything promised in the Word of God now becomes ours by faith.

Salvation is so much more than what I call "fire insurance." It includes peace, wholeness, well-being, prosperity, joy, divine health, and more. Fear is not something we have to tolerate at all when we understand our covenant. God will not break any promises He makes to us; His Word is infallible.

Hebrews 2:14-16 explains covenant freedom from fear even further:

> *Forasmuch then as the children are partakers of flesh and blood, he also himself likewise took part of the same; that through death he might destroy him that had the power of death, that is, the devil; And deliver them who through fear of death were all their lifetime subject to bondage. For verily he took not on him the nature of angels; but he took on him the seed of Abraham.*

Satan uses fear to torment people and ultimately kill them because he knows fear is a spiritual principle that will work for anyone who will get involved with it. In fact, even more than his concern about whether we go to heaven or hell is his preoccupation with getting us out of his way completely. But Jesus did something so powerful on the cross; He actually *destroyed* Satan and delivered us from the power of death, which comes through fear. When we come into covenant with God through Jesus, we are no longer subject to the torment and bondage of fear. Jesus has paid the price for us to be free from it.

FEAR TOLERATED IS FAITH CONTAMINATED

We must settle the trust issue between ourselves and God if we want to see the promises of the covenant come to pass. The life of faith says, "I trust and believe in God, no matter what." It doesn't believe the circumstances more than it does the promise. It is the same attitude Abraham had, even when he hadn't yet seen the manifestation of what God told him.

> "GOD WANTS HIS COVENANT TO BECOME A PART OF OUR SPIRITUAL SYSTEM."

Faith is vital because everything in the Kingdom of God operates by it. The Bible says it is impossible to please God without it. Our healing, victory, peace, and freedom from fear depend on our faith, and it all starts with a quality decision to make God's Word the final authority in our lives. With that being said, we must know that when we tolerate fear in any form, we contaminate our faith and short-circuit everything God is trying to do for us.

Since fear and faith operate by the same principles and are supernatural "connectors," Satan knows there is nothing he can do to change the way things work. So what he tries to do is contaminate our faith by getting us to focus on the things we should take authority over. If a Christian is doing all the right things according to the Word, and is still not connecting to the full manifestation of the promise, the issue may be that there is fear present that is not being dealt with. We must look at our lives and locate areas where fear is operating, even if these areas seem insignificant. Any fear, if left to its own devices, will contaminate your faith in God's Word.

Sometimes we even pray fear-based prayers and then we wonder why they aren't being answered. When we come to God, we must come from a position of boldness and righteousness, without fear, doubt, inferiority, or condemnation. If any of these things are present when we make our requests known to the Lord, we are hindering our prayers.

Taffi and I had to make a decision to fear-proof our home, particularly since this was an area in which the enemy was attacking us. We decided that fear would not be a part of our lives because it would give Satan the avenue he needs to destroy everything we are trying to accomplish. It was a choice that had to be developed and cultivated daily.

In becoming stronger in our choice to not allow our faith to be contaminated by fear, we had to develop our confidence by acting on what the Word says rather than our feelings. Faith is a practical expression of our confidence in God and His Word, so when we choose to rise above fear by not acting in compliance with it, we are "de-contaminating" our faith.

For example, if you have a fear of being home alone at night like Taffi did, you can choose to do one of two things: act out on that fear and perpetuate it, or do something that defies the fear through a practical expression of your confidence in God's Word. Turning all the lights on in the house and not going to sleep when you are home alone are acts of fear. Can you imagine the mental bondage a person endures to stay awake late at night, even though he or she may be exhausted and sleepy, simply because he or she is afraid to sleep in an empty house at night? That's no way to live.

So instead of giving in to the fear by staying up and turning on every light in the house, actively engage your faith by declaring the Word of God, which says He gives His beloved sleep and that you possess power, love, and a sound mind instead of fear. Then turn off those lights and go to bed!

Another example is in the area of finances. Many times, the enemy will attempt to get us to focus more on our current circumstances than on the promises of God where finances are concerned. However, provision is a covenant guarantee. If it looks like you don't have enough in your bank account to cover you bills for the month, remain committed to not walk in fear. Instead, meditate and speak the Word of God concerning your finances and do something bold to counter the fear and demonstrate your faith in God. Sow a seed in church, or give to someone in need, believing that what you give will be given back to you pressed down, shaken together, and running over. Every act of faith on your part keeps your faith free of contamination.

Keeping your faith pure of all defilement is going to take effort on your part. You must do something to resist any attacks on a consistent basis. When it comes to fear, you can't afford to take a lackadaisical attitude. It is a force that must be pushed back. I will even go so far as to say that fear is afraid of your resistance. So the moment you refuse to allow it to contaminate your faith, it will leave. It has no choice but to yield and submit to the blood of Jesus and the authority of His name.

BUILDING CONFIDENCE IN THE COVENANT

Building your confidence in the covenant God has made with you doesn't happen overnight. This is something that takes time and repetition. It begins with picking up your Bible and spending time in it every day. Just like your body needs food to function properly, your spirit needs the nourishment of God's Word to remain strong and less susceptible to fear. For me, I found that "rehearsing" the Word every day was the key to getting rid of fear and building up my faith.

What does it mean to "rehearse" the Word? It is taking the Word and reading it and turning it over in your mind repeatedly. It involves speaking the Word all the time. When you rehearse something, it will eventually become like second nature. It won't be long before you won't even think about it anymore; faith will be an automatic response to the situations that confront you. Confidence is born out of rehearsing the Word of God.

God wants His covenant to become a part of our spiritual system. Similar to a computer that is programmed with certain software, Believers must program themselves with the Word of God. All the discipline, practice, and attention we give to its principles will keep us on track. All of a sudden, we will wake up one day and realize we don't even know how to fear anymore, and all we know how to do is operate by faith!

Satan doesn't have a right to do anything to us because of our covenant with God and our position of righteousness in Him. The question is, do you believe that? Do you believe you have been redeemed from the curse of living a fear-filled life? Hebrews 10:35 instructs to not cast away our confidence because there is a great reward attached to placing our trust in God. He guarantees that when we walk by faith, we will see the manifestation of what we believe.

I want to encourage you to examine your life and ask the Holy Spirit to reveal any fear you have that you may not be aware of. It may be where relationships are concerned, or in the areas of finances or health. It may be something no one even knows about but you. The key is to identify it and locate a promise in God's Word that covers that fear. Rehearse your faith and resist fear with everything in you. Stand on the covenant of God, knowing that you have *already* been redeemed from the attacks of the enemy. Your confidence in God will connect you to your covenant benefits!

CHAPTER 5
Refuse to Worry

"Therefore I say unto you, Take no thought for your life, what ye
Shall eat, or what ye shall drink; nor yet for your body, what ye
shall put on. Is not the life more than meat,
and the body than raiment?"

(Matthew 6:25).

Have you ever become so consumed with the cares of life that you just couldn't seem to stop thinking about them? When you give so much mental energy to those concerns that you begin to constantly worry, you have opened the door to the enemy. Some people believe worry is a natural, uncontrollable emotion that is an inevitable part of life. Actually, worry is nothing more than one of the many faces of fear. We understand that fear does not come from God; He is not the author of it, and anything that is not from God should not be tolerated in our lives.

When you get right down to it, worry does nothing to change our situations and circumstances, but, instead, it perpetuates the very fears we don't want to come to pass.

Sometimes it seems we just can't stop worrying, but the truth is we *can* take authority over it. We *choose* to either worry or trust God. By meditating on the Word more than we do the problem, however, we can overcome worry.

I view worry in the same way I do a nagging pain somewhere on the body that isn't necessarily incapacitating, but is present nonetheless. The fact that you've grown used to it, and that it isn't at the forefront of your thinking all the time doesn't mean it's healthy or that you don't need to get the problem resolved. Likewise, we can get so used to worrying that it becomes a way of life.

WORRY, A PLATFORM FOR SATAN

In order for Satan to operate against us, we must have fear; however, where there is no fear, he cannot function. By the same token, God needs faith to operate, and without it, we shouldn't expect to receive anything from Him. Worry is simply negative meditation. It is when we meditate on the words of the devil more than we do the Word of God. The Lord wants us to live fear-free lives, but we paralyze His power when we get into fear through worry. When we worry, we are essentially doubting God's ability to handle the situation.

The greatest fear Satan wants to inflict upon Believers is the fear that what God promised in His Word won't come to pass. His entire objective is to get us to doubt the Word and abandon our faith. He accomplishes this by speaking to our hearts and minds and getting us to focus on his negative words. Then, once the process of worry begins, if left unchecked, it will ultimately lead us right into the manifestation of what we are worrying about.

How does worry get into our hearts? Through words. Romans 10:17 says, *"So then faith cometh by hearing, and hearing by the word of God."* According to this scripture, faith enters into our hearts by hearing the Word of God. But fear enters our hearts the same way—by hearing the words of the enemy and receiving them. This is the starting point for worry.

If there's one thing I see in the lives of so many people, it is worry. From how the bills are going to get paid to where the next meal is coming from, worry has become the norm for so many Believers. Some people are what I like to call

> "...WORRY IS NOTHING MORE THAN ONE OF THE MANY FACES OF FEAR."

"professional worriers." They don't even understand what they are participating in, and how their fears are actually causing negative things to take place in their lives. As a result, they continue to worry and never deal with it.

It is absolutely devastating to a person's life to never get an understanding of the destruction that worry can cause. If you are one of those people who looks at the news and begins to worry about anything and everything that is going on around you, it's time to break the habit! The Word of God is the answer.

THE POWER OF MEDITATION

When most people hear the word *meditation,* they think of being silent and still, emptying their minds of all thought, and just focusing on nothing at all. New Age religions often promote meditation as the path to achieving a higher state of "consciousness." However, this is actually not what true meditation is. We only achieve a higher state of consciousness through the Word of God. When we meditate, we shouldn't "empty" our minds of all thoughts because this creates a mental environment that is ripe for the enemy to plant his seeds of fear. True meditation is actually an active thought process that engages all of our focus and attention.

To *meditate* on something means to ponder, consider, think about, and roll it over in your mind again and again. It also means to mutter or repeat. With this basic understanding of meditation, it becomes clear how it can apply to negative or positive thoughts.

Joshua 1:8 instructs us to meditate on the Word of God day and night so we can make our way prosperous in life and have good success. When you continually think about and ponder the Word, it won't be long before that Word will begin speaking to you. You will begin to hear the *voice* of God behind the Scriptures, which will give you the specific directions you need for your situation. This is what real meditation is all about. It produces results in your life, not just an empty state of mind.

Now, worry, on the other hand, is the reciprocal of godly, faith-filled meditation. When you are worrying, you are meditating on the contradictions to the Word of God. It is *negative meditation.*

When you worry, you are pondering the negative thought and rolling it around in your mind, which will eventually lead you to speak the things you are worrying about. Before long you are a participant in the tragedy you helped create.

Meditation is so powerful because it is part of the creative ability with which God has gifted all of us. Words produce mindsets and our mindsets influence our emotions. If we are feeling depressed, fearful, and negatively concerned about our futures, it is because of what we have been meditating on. If you want to change the way you feel, change the way you think, which begins with dealing with the words you are giving your attention to.

Besides connecting us to the things we are worrying about, another reason why God doesn't want us to meditate on the negative rather than the positive is because it causes us to crown ourselves as "god" over our situations. Oftentimes, people think they are taking control over their circumstances by worrying about them, when in reality they are making the situations worse. It is like telling God, "You can't do this, so I'm going to hold on to the care of this situation." It demonstrates that we don't trust the Lord with the details of our lives.

Being a pastor, there are so many things I encounter and have encountered over the years that would cause most people to buckle. We have to believe God to take care of our needs, just like anyone else! Not to mention, we also have to trust the Lord to handle all the details and needs of the ministry. Over the years, we have been faced with challenging financial situations that have pushed our faith to the limit. In those moments of pressure, we had to ultimately choose who we would trust—God or ourselves. Worry could have easily taken over our thought processes, but we had to let it go and let God take over. Every time we chose faith over fear, the situation turned around and worked out in our favor.

Philippians 1:28 says, *"And in nothing terrified by your adversaries: which is to them an evident token of perdition, but to you of salvation, and that of God."* What a loaded scripture! First, it says *"And in nothing terrified..."* I'm sure you've been faced with situations that could be considered terrifying. Whether it is a financial crisis, a physical illness, or concern about a loved one, there is always something in our lives the enemy will use to try to scare us. However, fear has no platform to stand on when we allow the Word of God to minister to us more than the words of Satan. This scripture promises that when we stand before our adversaries, whether they are actual people or negative circumstances, we will *not* be terrified.

Second, when we refuse to fear, something powerful happens. In the Amplified Bible, verse 28 says, *"...such constancy and fearlessness will be a clear sign (proof and seal) to them of [their impending] destruction, but [a sure token and evidence] of your deliverance and salvation, and that from God."* When the enemy does everything he can to put fear in our hearts and get us to worry, our stance on the Word of God is what will cause those fearful situations, and even people in some cases, to be removed. The confidence in this promise comes through constant meditation of what God has said.

What do you do in the midst of challenges? Do you allow yourself to become intimidated and fearful? Do you start praising God in the midst of it, or do you complain and turn your back on God's Word? The attitude with which you attack negative situations determines the outcome. You have to let the devil know who's going to win the battle!

DAVID'S ATTITUDE

King David is a great example of how a victorious attitude in the face of battle can put you over the top. Throughout his life, David faced some serious challenges. If there is anyone who could have had reason to worry, it was him! Many times David had those closest to him turn on him, even to the point of his own family trying to kill him. Many of the chapters in the Book of Psalms were written by David while he was on the run from his enemies. However, his strength, courage, tenacity, and faith in God kept him going. He meditated on the Word so that worry would not overtake him.

The account of David and Goliath (1 Samuel 17) particularly stands out as a story about the power of fearlessness. David knew his covenant with God, and it empowered him to defeat an enemy who was ten times larger and stronger than he was from a physical perspective. I don't know about you, but if I were facing a giant who was ready to crush me to death, the temptation to worry would definitely be present! David didn't buckle for one moment, though. He never spoke one word of doubt or unbelief. He never expressed worry about the outcome of the fight. He *knew* God's delivering power was at work on his behalf.

At the outset of the contest, David asked, *"What shall be done to the man who killeth this Philistine, and taketh away the reproach from Israel? For who is this uncircumcised Philistine, that he should defy the armies of the living God?"* Clearly David had a confident attitude going into this thing. Further along in the chapter, Goliath declares to him, *"Come to me, and I will give thy flesh unto the fowls of the air, and to the beasts of the field."* To stand in the face of such threats without fear or worry would take courage. David simply replied, *"Thou comest to me with a sword, and with a spear, and with a shield: but I come to thee in the name of the Lord of hosts, the God of the armies of Israel, who thou hast defied"* (v. 45).

See, David didn't have fear, and on top of that the Word says he *ran* toward Goliath (v. 48)! He actually went after the challenge in faith, released his rock, hit his target, and defeated his enemy. By focusing on God more than the problem, the challenge was eliminated.

HE HAS YOUR BACK

One of the areas in which people really deal with this issue of worry is where getting their needs met is concerned. News reports of a dragging economy and a host of other societal problems can easily get into your head if you are not mindful to guard against them. We live in a time where meditating and focusing on the Word of God is more important than ever. Our lives literally depend on it.

Jesus had some very encouraging words to share in Matthew 6:25-32 pertaining to our daily needs. When we really grab hold of these scriptures it will revolutionize our faith and trust in God. He says:

> *Therefore I say unto you, Take no thought for your life, what ye shall eat, or what ye shall drink; nor yet for your body, what ye shall put on. Is not the life more than meat, and the body than raiment? Behold the fowls of the air: for they sow not, neither do they reap, nor gather into barns; yet your heavenly Father feedeth them. Are ye not much better than they? Which of you by taking thought can add one cubit unto his stature? And why take ye thought for raiment? Consider the lilies of the field, how they grow; they toil not, neither do they spin: And yet I say unto you, That even Solomon in all his glory was not arrayed like one of these. Wherefore, if God so clothe the grass of the field, which today is, and tomorrow is cast into the oven, shall he not much more clothe you, O ye of little faith? Therefore take no thought, saying, What shall we eat? or, What shall we drink? or, Wherewithal shall we be clothed? (For after all these things do the Gentiles seek:) for your heavenly Father knoweth that ye have need of all these things.*

Everything in this passage is dealing with our daily necessities, which are things people tend to strive for and seek after. But God is saying, "*Don't worry about those things; I've got you covered! If I take care of the birds and the flowers of the field, how much more will I take care of you?*"

The Amplified version of verse 25 says, "*Therefore I tell you, stop being perpetually uneasy (anxious and worried) about your life, what you shall eat or what you shall drink; or about your body, what you shall put on...*" I'm sure you can think of times where you were "perpetually uneasy and anxious" about something or worrying about how your needs were going to be met. Jesus instructs us to "take no thought" about these things because He has us covered. He is well able to provide for us in every area of our lives, including food, clothing, and shelter.

TAKING THOUGHTS INVOLVES WORDS

I want you to notice that Jesus said "take no thought, *saying...*," which means the way we "take" thoughts is through speaking words. It's kind of like signing for a package at your front door. We take worry when we talk about the problem and rehearse it out loud. Every time we speak words that affirm the challenge, we are taking the negative thoughts of the enemy and perpetuating a cycle of worry. God doesn't want us to speak about things we are afraid of or worried about because our words authorize the devil to get involved.

Refusing to take worrisome thoughts is a simple decision that will do wonders for our faith. God isn't going to force us to refuse to worry; we must do it as an act of our wills. Imagining every possible negative outcome will form the blueprint for those things to come to pass. That is why I can't emphasize enough the importance of executing 2 Corinthians 10:5 when negative thoughts come and try to exalt themselves above the Word of God. They must be dealt with quickly and aggressively. Casting down thoughts means speaking the Word of God boldly and authoritatively *as soon as the thoughts come.* When you are in the middle of a thought and you say something, that thought is captured. An exercise you can do to prove this is true is to count to ten in your mind and then say your name in the midst of your counting. Your words will stop what is going on in your mind.

When you feel fear trying to manifest itself in your mind through worry, this is not the time to remain silent. Open your mouth and declare the Word of God. Stop being perpetually uneasy and anxious about the things that concern you! Jesus already knew your needs before you were even aware of them.

Remember, there is no increase that comes from worry, except in the negative; it won't change anything for the better, but only for the worse. Worrying supports Satan's agenda, which is why you must grit your teeth and fight the urge to give in to it. Meditate on God's Word until that Word becomes more real to you than the problem. Positive meditation will drive out fear. Most of all, you must commit to allowing God to be your source. He will provide everything you need and more.

Brother Kenneth Hagin, a great man of faith, once said

something that resonates in my life where thoughts are concerned. He said, "You can't stop the birds from flying over your head, but you can stop them from building a nest in your hair." In other words, there are certain thoughts that are going to go through your head, but you just have to make sure you don't allow those thoughts to settle in permanently in your mind. Don't sign for the package of worry. If you find yourself in a situation that looks hopeless, spend time in the Word of God and agree with what God has already said about your life. Praise Him and trust Him rather than worrying. Your answer is one scripture away!

CHAPTER 6
Doubt: A Faith Killer

"But let him ask in faith, nothing wavering. For he that wavereth is like a wave of sea driven with the wind and tossed. For let not that man think that he shall receive any thing of the Lord"

(James 1:8).

If there is one thing that will absolutely destroy our faith and keep the promises of God out of reach, it is doubt. You may not realize it, but doubt is another way fear shows its ugly face. All my life, I heard about doubt, but I never made the connection between doubt and fear, or just how counterproductive it really is. It is something that must be dealt with so our faith can work at an optimum level.

There is nothing natural about fear, and while it may exist in people's hearts and minds, it does not originate from God, who is the author of all natural things. Since 2 Timothy 1:7 says God does not give us the spirit of fear, we know it must come from somewhere else. We also know that if we put up with fear in any form, our faith will be contaminated.

Fear comes from the outside; it is a spirit that attacks our minds and emotions, and works to move us out of God's will for our lives. It comes through words, images, and suggestions the enemy makes to our minds. Now, what happens when a person doesn't know what the Word of God says? Well, he or she is open to things that contradict the Bible. People who don't know the Word will be deceived and taken advantage of by the enemy. He will plant fear in their hearts, and they will have more confidence in the contradiction to the Word than in what God says. A mind that is governed by the contradictions is susceptible to doubt.

FAITH TO STAND IN A WORLD OF DOUBT

I believe now, more than ever before, we must wake up to the truth of God's Word and put our faith and trust in the Lord. We are living in the last days—a time in which deception is running rampant. People are turning away from God in record numbers, including those who were once strong Believers! The secular humanist mindset that is prevalent throughout the world is creating an atmosphere that promotes doubt in God's Word. As Christians, we must be sure to remain grounded in faith, in the midst of everything going on around us.

Webster's Dictionary defines *doubt* as, "to be uncertain or unsure; to tend to distrust or disbelieve; a lack of certainty or conviction; and uncertain state of affairs." Another way I define it is, "a highly concentrated thought on the contradiction to the Word." When we doubt, we are not fully convinced that the Word works, is real, or will come to pass. It is that place of uncertainty that keeps us from really making a complete decision to believe, which is what God requires.

So how does doubt enter our hearts? I wish I could give you some overly spiritual answer, but it really is as simple as what you give your attention to. Faith needs to be fed in order to be strong, and we do this by filling ourselves up with God's Word and continually meditating on it. Similarly, doubt must also be fed in order for it to take precedence in your life. If you give your attention to the world's way of thinking, which puts no validity or stock in the things of God, don't expect for your faith to be strong. If you hang around people who don't believe in the Bible and focus your attention on secular beliefs, you simply won't believe what God says is true.

If we are to stand in the face of the world's doubt and negative attitude toward God, the Bible, and anything that represents Christianity, we must be faith giants. We've got to make our minds up that *nothing* is going to stand between us and God's promises. We cannot allow doubt to rob us of what rightfully belongs to us, whether it is healing, deliverance, or financial increase. Getting our faith to this level is going to cost us something, meaning we can't expect to have mountain-moving faith if we're not willing to do what is necessary to build ourselves up spiritually. God is waiting on us to come to Him so He can empower us with the tools we need to win.

HOW DOUBT GETS IN

There is a specific eight-step process by which we end up at a particular destination. It begins with the words we receive in our minds, which shape our thoughts. Our thoughts lead to how we feel; our feelings cause us to take action; our actions lead to habits; our habits create our character; and our character ultimately takes us to our destination. Satan uses doubt to get us to a destination of failure. Because he knows God needs our faith to bring His will to pass in our lives, he starts his attack in our minds, by trying to get us to receive words of doubt and unbelief.

I am sure you've had the experience of being confronted with a principle or promise from the Bible and doubting it was true or that it would work for you at first. The doubt didn't just get there haphazardly; it came because of *words* the enemy spoke to your mind. Words like, *"You don't believe that do you?" "How could that be possible?" "That kind of thing doesn't happen in the real world,"* or *"How do you expect God to do that?"*

> "A MIND THAT IS GOVERNED BY THE CONTRADICTIONS IS SUSCEPTIBLE TO DOUBT."

Satan will speak directly to our minds, especially when we are confronted by situations that look impossible to us.

Another avenue the enemy uses to speak doubt into our hearts and minds is through other people. This is why it is so vital that you consult only with the Word of God and other strong, faith-filled Christians who believe the Bible wholeheartedly. If you pay attention to what you can perceive with your senses or talk to friends and family who have embraced the world's way of thinking, you can be sure that you will begin to doubt the supernatural power of God.

When it comes to overcoming doubt, the truth is, the things of the spirit must be more real to you than even what you see with your eyes. But this won't happen if you listen to people who are full of doubt and unbelief. The fool says in his heart, *"There is no God."* If you sit and listen to a fool, you will start thinking like one, and believe me, this way of thinking will pull your faith down faster than you can imagine.

Once those words of doubt are spoken, and you do not immediately deal with them, they will begin to shape the way you think. The more you hear, the more your mind will be influenced in a negative way. As a result of that doubting mindset, you will begin to feel strongly that God's way of doing things is a waste of time. Doubt will then move you to do things that don't line up with the Word. You'll start speaking and acting in a way that demonstrates you do not believe the Scriptures. You'll start trusting in man's ability, and your own ability, apart from God. This is why the Bible says, "Keep thy heart with all diligence, for out of it are the issues of life" (Proverbs 4:23).

If you don't want to go in the direction of doubt, it's going to be critical that you screen every word you hear and every image you look at by holding it up against the Word of God and judging it based on that standard. The battle of faith is won or lost in the arena of the mind, and if you don't know how to be a good custodian over your thought life, you'll be bombarded with doubt that is designed to derail your faith.

So we must take authority over our minds, begin to meditate on the Word at every available opportunity, and get into the habit of casting down thoughts of doubt and unbelief by declaring the truths found in the Scriptures. For example, when the thought comes, *"I doubt I'm going to be able to pay my bills,"* you say, *"My God shall supply all of my needs according to His riches in glory."* When you doubt God's ability to heal you of a disease or infirmity, open your mouth and declare, *"By the stripes of Jesus Christ I am healed! His blood has been shed. I'm not moved by how I feel, I'm moved by faith. I'm moved by the Word of God."* By doing this, you protect your mind from doubt's debilitating effects. The last thing you say is the last thing you will think.

TAKE ACTION

When it comes to believing God's Word, it isn't enough to just *say* you believe. Real, Bible-based belief is demonstrated by what we *do*. Every Sunday, people who are supposed to be *Believers* come to church, hear a life-changing message preached, go home, and fail every test the enemy throws their way. Many times the tests are failed before they even leave the church parking lot! When do we get to the point that our belief in God's Word moves us to actually execute the information and revelation we receive at church? Belief is only belief at the point of execution.

If you don't believe the Word to the point of actually doing it, then fearing that the Word really doesn't work is present in your life. Remember, doubt is about not trusting God. So when you hear something from the Word and you fail to execute it, you give Satan permission to carry out his will in your life.

You may wonder how big a deal doubt is in God's eyes. Revelation 21:8 couples fear and unbelief, and also categorizes these two mindsets with those who will *"have their part in the lake which burneth with fire and brimstone."* From a heavenly perspective, doubt is just as bad as murder or sexual immorality. That's because it aims for the very heart of what activates the Kingdom of God—faith. Fear and unbelief go together; you can't have one without the other, which is how you know doubt is a manifestation of fear.

DOUBT NOT

God is calling us to a place of absolute faith in Him. But it is going to require our courage and commitment. James 1:6 says, *"But let him ask in faith, nothing wavering. For he that wavereth is like a wave of sea driven with the wind and tossed. For let not that man think that he shall receive any thing of the Lord."* When we have doubt and unbelief, we are no different from a wave being tossed to and fro by the wind, and God says this person shouldn't expect to receive anything from Him.

Jesus' disciples struggled with doubt at various times during their journey with the Lord during His earthly ministry. One of the most noted accounts of the disciples having to extend their faith in the Lord was when they saw Him walking on the tumultuous waves of the sea. Matthew 14:22-31 describes what happened:

> And straightway Jesus constrained his disciples to get into a ship, and to go before him unto the other side, while he sent the multitude away. And when he had sent the multitudes away, he went up into a mountain apart to pray: and when the evening was come, he was there alone. But the ship was now in the midst of the sea, tossed with waves: for the wind was contrary. And in the fourth watch of the night Jesus went unto them, walking on the sea. And when the disciples saw him walking on the sea, they were troubled, saying, It is a spirit; and they cried out in fear. But straightway Jesus spake unto them, saying, Be of good cheer; it is I; be not afraid. And Peter answered him and said, Lord, if it be thou, bid me come unto thee on the water. And he said, Come, And when Peter was come down out of the ship, he walked on the water, to go to Jesus. But when he saw the wind boisterous, he was afraid, and beginning to sink, he cried, saying, Lord, save me. And immediately Jesus stretched forth his hand, and caught him, and said unto him, O thou of little faith, wherefore didst thou doubt?

In this passage, we see Jesus, whom the disciples had relationship with and had seen perform great miracles, doing something supernatural—He was defying natural laws by walking on water. But this was no different from any other supernatural act they had witnessed. In fact, they had *just* seen Jesus multiply fish and bread to feed five thousand people! However, the disciples struggled with doubt, and in these moments, their faith in exactly who was approaching them was wavering as they began to allow fear into their thinking.

Peter decided to take a chance and step out of the boat. Jesus, in response to his faith, said: "*Come.*" Peter was the only disciple who dared to believe the Lord in those critical moments, and as a result of his faith, he was also able to defy natural laws and walk on the water toward Jesus. The problem came when Peter began to pay attention to what was going on around him—the wind, the waves, and the atmosphere of tumultuous weather. At the very moment that he gave his attention to his surroundings, doubt entered his mind, and he began to sink.

How many times have we decided to walk on the water, and even stepped out on faith, only to have doubt and fear creep into our hearts because of contradicting circumstances? Or, have we become like the rest of the disciples who dared not step out of the boat at all because of their doubt and unbelief? Jesus said Peter had "little" faith because it only lasted for a brief moment before he allowed doubt to quench it. It was a short burst of faith that had no endurance. That's what doubt's job is—to deflate your faith so it can't go the distance. Fear of sinking connected Peter to the thing he feared, and doubt contaminated his faith.

The same thing happens to us when we start giving our attention to the contradictions to God's Word. Jesus told Peter to "Come," and the devil said, "Wind blow." Like Peter, we may have a tendency to give the words of the enemy a second thought, but we must keep our faith guns locked and loaded at all times. If Peter had opened his mouth and declared the Word of God in that situation, I'm sure he would have continued his "water walk" toward Jesus with no problems!

Second Timothy 3:1 says that in the last days, perilous times will come. This prophecy includes the attack on faith that the devil is launching against Christians everywhere. There are all kinds of things being pumped through the media to try to get us to doubt the infallibility of the Bible. From historical documentaries on television that seek to discredit the Word of God to popular entertainment icons who influence the mindsets of the public away from God's way of doing things, all of it is designed to get us to take a "second" thought. Whom will you give your attention to? Whom will you believe?

There is a lot of false teaching out there, and deception is on the rise, but Taffi and I made a decision long ago to stick with the Word of God. It is the only thing we can depend on. Anything that does not line up with the Bible must be discarded and ignored if we are to keep our faith levels high and our doubt levels low.

Every contradiction is wrapped up in a package designed to get you to question the validity of what God says. I encourage you to examine your life and take inventory of any areas where doubt and unbelief have crept in. Has the enemy used the circumstances around you to set you up for the second thought? Maybe an unexpected bill came in or you are experiencing pain in your body. How you handle those moments determines whether you see the situation turn around or not. If doubt tries to attack your mind, capture the thought with the Word of God and declare the truth. Refuse to give Satan any room in your mind. If you are a Believer, purpose to believe the first thought, which is what comes from God's Word. Feed your faith and starve your doubts!

CHAPTER 7
Anger: Fear in Action

"But let him ask in faith, nothing wavering. For he that wavereth is like a wave of sea driven with the wind and tossed. For let not that man think that he shall receive any thing of the Lord"

(James 1:8).

Did you know that fear doesn't just manifest as an overwhelming concern about danger or catastrophe taking place? There are other ways it shows up, which most people have no idea are actually connected. Fear is a spirit that comes from Satan and is designed to draw us into his plans and purposes for our lives. Many times, we don't realize that when we have negative emotional responses to people and situations, those feelings are actually fueled by some type of deep-rooted fear that we may not even be aware of. Dealing with fear at the root level is a liberating key to overcoming anger and hurt.

If there is anyone who knows firsthand about the emotion of anger, I do. Over the years, I have learned to control my temper and walk in the love of God, but there was a time when anger ruled my life and responses to certain situations. It began to cause such stress in my life that I realized I had to do something about it or my health would even be compromised. As I continued my journey with God and began to get more revelation about the spirit of fear, I realized that fear is actually at the root of anger.

The area of finances is probably one of the most prevalent ones to prompt angry reactions, particularly between spouses. When the money is "funny" or when one spouse spends money in a way the other disapproves of, it can cause sparks to fly. For example, a man's wife might go to the mall and use one of the credit cards to go shopping. If she buys several items and tells her husband about it later, he may react in anger to her shopping spree.

Does the fact that she went shopping warrant such an emotional outburst from him? While he may be angry with his wife for using the card, that's not really the root to his response. The real issue is fear. Most likely, deep down, he has a fear of financial lack. Her shopping spree only brought that fear to the surface, causing him to go into a panic mode. He might not immediately tell his wife what is really bothering him, but the truth is that he fears running out of money.

We have all encountered situations where anger bubbled up from within us, and we dismissed it once we cooled off and exchanged apologies. But when fear is present, and not dealt with, it will cause these types of emotions to show up again and again. Anytime we get angry, we need to ask ourselves, "Is there an area of fear present that I may not be aware of?" If there is, we should ask the Holy Spirit to reveal it to us.

TWO KINDS OF ANGER

Emotions are feelings on the inside designed to move us in a certain direction. Anger is an interesting emotion because it can achieve vastly different outcomes, depending on how it is channeled. Not all anger is destructive; in fact, anger can be used to propel us toward the things of God in a more dynamic way when we recognize the difference between godly and ungodly anger.

Everyone gets angry—even God. The Bible mentions numerous times when the Lord's anger was kindled. He was angered by Israel's disobedience and stubborn rebellion many times. The Word says that He may get angry for a moment, but He doesn't stay angry. That's comforting to know!

Even Jesus got angry about the things people were doing at that time. The Scriptures recount how He drove moneychangers out of the synagogue because they were turning the place of worship into a "den of thieves" (Mark 11:15-17). Can you imagine how upset Jesus would have been to turn over tables and run people out of the church? The difference between God's anger and the anger of most of us experience, however, is that His anger is driven by righteousness and a hatred for sin. It is what can be called holy indignation. It is what moves Him to take action in a way that ultimately results in the preservation of His Word and way of doing things. His anger is actually a manifestation of His loving desire for people to live the life He intends. God knows we can't achieve this abundant life when sin and disobedience are in the way.

And yet, the Word of God talks about another kind of anger that we must guard against. It is the kind that turns to bitterness, gets in our hearts, and defiles us. It is the anger which Ephesians 4:26 speaks of and warns, *"When angry, do not sin; do not ever let your wrath (your exasperation, your fury or indignation) last until the sun goes down. Leave no [such] room or foothold for the devil [give no opportunity to him]."* This type of anger is usually fear-based and has the potential to do great damage to our relationships if left unchecked.

I like to use the example of fire to describe anger. Fire, by itself, is not an enemy. In fact, when contained in the right setting, it can be a great benefit, providing warmth and even the ability to cook food. However, fire does have the potential to do a lot of damage if it is not handled appropriately, or if it is used in the wrong way. When it gets out of control it can kill. Likewise, when anger is inappropriately channeled, and is driven by fear and self-preservation, it can become a destructive force.

Fear-based anger can easily become rage. The increased frequency of school and office shootings is a testament to the fear and anger that is running rampant in society. When fear is behind rage, abuse and destruction is inevitable. The enemy will begin speaking to people, telling them that by hurting others they are somehow protecting themselves or issuing some type of justice for the hurt and pain they have personally suffered.

Such extreme outbursts of anger and violence toward others really have fear at the root. Feeling the need to control another person through brute force is based on inferiority and is nothing more than a manifestation of fear. Consequently, a person who is driven by fear to this level will ultimately use fear as a tactic to terrorize and intimidate others. It is a vicious cycle that must be broken.

IDENTIFYING FEAR-BASED ANGER

When I think about fear-based anger and the extent to which it can drive people, what comes to my mind is the conflict between Jesus and the religious leaders of His day. The Pharisees and Sadducees were full of hatred for Jesus because He challenged their religious traditions and beliefs. The Gospel He preached was one of love, not based on the religious bondage of the Law, which was what they followed to the letter. His message was one of healing, hope, and freedom in a world and culture where religious traditions were held as the highest standard of what it meant to be connected to God.

There are numerous accounts of the Pharisees being angry with Jesus, but the real issue is that they were *afraid* of Him. He came on the scene with teachings and declarations about the Father that they weren't prepared to deal with or receive. The controversial nature of His teachings posed a problem for them because it meant there was a possibility they could lose control of the people who followed their way of doing things. Jesus was a threat to the status quo. These men were full of pride, and their fear drove them to silence Jesus at all costs, even if it meant killing Him.

One particular passage of scripture really shows how their fear drove them to extreme anger and rage toward Jesus. John 10:30-39 says:

> *I and my Father are one. Then the Jews took up stones again to stone him. Jesus answered them, Many good works have I shown you from my Father; for which of those works do ye stone me? The Jews answered him, saying, For a good work we stone thee not; but for blasphemy; and because that thou, being a man, makest thyself God. Jesus answered them, Is it not written in your law, I said, Ye are gods? If he called them gods, unto whom the word of God came, and the scripture cannot be broken; Say ye of him, whom the Father hath sanctified, and sent into the world, Thou blasphemest; because I said, I am the Son of God? If I do not the works of my Father, believe me not. But if I do, though ye believe not me, believe the works: that ye may know, and believe, that the Father is in me, and I in him. Therefore they sought again to take him: but he escaped out of their hand...*

The Pharisees didn't have a revelation of who Jesus was, so they couldn't accept His claims to be one with the Father.

Another passage says they actually tried to throw Him off a cliff, but He was able to slip out of their grasp. Their anger toward Jesus was completely fear-based.

I think the example of the Pharisees' behavior proves that anger, when it is based in fear, and is left unchecked, can drive a person to act out in violent and destructive ways. It is often not until after the fact that they realize how they allowed the enemy to use them for his purposes. It becomes clear why a "little" fear is *never* okay.

> "DEALING WITH FEAR AT THE ROOT LEVEL IS A LIBERATING KEY TO OVERCOMING ANGER AND HURT."

Dealing with fear-based anger requires the application of God's Word. We must recognize that anytime we are offended, insulted, or feel threatened, Satan has an avenue into our minds and hearts. When we encounter these negative emotions, we have to identify them as being fear-based and deal with them immediately by taking authority over them.

LOVE IS THE ANSWER

When it comes to getting rid of fear-based anger, the antidote is love. First John 4:18 says, *"There is no fear in love; but perfect love casteth out fear: because fear hath torment. He that feareth is not made perfect in love."* When we walk in any kind of fear, it is evidence of a deficiency in our love walk. But when we perfect the love of God in us, it flushes fear out of our spirits.

Fear and love cannot be in the presence of the other.

You may be wondering how to "perfect" the love of God in your life. First, perfected love means mature love. Every day we will have opportunities to exercise love toward others. There will always be a "love test" awaiting our response. It could be a difficult co-worker or family member. It may be a situation that arises between you and your spouse, or even with someone you encounter out in public. People will challenge us to grow by putting us in situations that force us to either choose love or selfishness. When we make a decision to walk in love before the situation arises, we will be prepared for it.

In addition to walking in love, we can also get rid of fear by immersing ourselves in God's presence through prayer and the meditation of His Word. The presence of God brings a level of security and comfort that absolutely drives fear out of the atmosphere. And when you get revelation of how much God loves you, fear will shrink.

First John 4:16 is a wonderful scripture to meditate on concerning the love of God, *"And we have known and believed the love that God hath to us. God is love; and he that dwelleth in love dwelleth in God, and God in him."* Knowing and believing in the love God has for us is critical to being free from fear. When we know He loves us, we can rest in the assurance that He has all our needs covered and that He will take care of us in *every* area. The love of God covers everything we will ever go through or deal with in life, whether it is relationships, finances, health, or emotional well-being. His love has the ability to fill the areas of our lives that are empty. Only His love can provide sustaining security.

If you feel fear has crept into your consciousness and is at the root of the anger you may experience, purpose to allow God's love to control your mind and spirit. Find scriptures that address the specific fear you are dealing with, and saturate yourself with His presence. When you know God loves you, your responses to life will change dramatically, and any anger based in fear will be a thing of the past.

CHAPTER 8
Dealing with the Fear of Lack

"For the Lord thy God hath blessed thee in all the works of thy hand: he knoweth thy walking through this great wilderness: these forty years the Lord thy God hath been with thee; thou hast lacked nothing"

(Deuteronomy 2:7).

There is no denying that the financial systems of this world are failing. You can turn on the television at any given time and see something about the economic problems that exist not only in our country but all over the world: Unemployment is at an all time high. The Dow Jones has fallen. Joblessness continues. Gas prices have gone up. Times have changed, and the truth of the matter is, they will continue to change right up until the return of the Lord. If we put our trust in the man-made institutions of this world system—such as the banks, social and political organizations, and even the government—we will quickly find ourselves on a path of despair and financial hardship. However, when we have a relationship with God and know Him as our only source of provision, we won't look to those institutions as our source, and the fear of lack won't rule our thinking.

I am convinced that the enemy has launched an all-out attack against faith through the avenue of the media. From a spiritual perspective, the things we see pumped through the television and Internet are designed for a specific purpose—to capitalize on and amplify fear in the hearts and minds of the general public. The more we pay attention to the news, the more fearful we become. As Believers, watching bad news on a consistent basis is probably one of the worst things we can do to our faith. Nothing will derail our trust in God quicker than filling our eyes and ears with the media's reports.

Financial lack is probably one of the most common fears that people deal with on a daily basis, and it also happens to be the issue we hear about regularly. It seems there is constant discussion about how bad things are, and how difficult it is for people to make it on a daily basis. To the average person, who has no knowledge about God's ability or willingness to provide for their needs, life is a rat race, in which the objective is basic survival. Consequently, people begin to see their jobs as a means to an end rather than a divine assignment, and the word that is used to describe their existence is *toil*. The fear of running out is what drives them to keep toiling, even if it is at the expense of their peace, sanity, health, and personal relationships.

For the person who chooses to trust in the Word of God where their provision is concerned, there is good news: It is not God's will for you to go through life toiling for your next meal or wondering how your bills are going to be paid. If you are a Believer, you have an unlimited source of supply. We know faith comes by hearing the Word of God, and fear comes from hearing the words of the devil. So if you find yourself being consumed with the fear of not having enough to meet your needs, you have to ask yourself, *What is it that I've been listening to?*

Have you been giving your attention to words that continue to provoke fear in your life? Are you turning the television on and hearing over and over again that businesses are closing and employment opportunities are becoming hard to find? By paying attention to such negative reports, you form a foundation for those fears to rest upon.

We know that Satan cannot operate in the life of a Believer unless he is given access through fear. Very simply put, where there is no fear, Satan is paralyzed. And by the same token, when you don't have faith, you put a hold on what God can do for you. If you find your faith wavering, it is a clear indication that fear is present. And when fear is present, so is unbelief.

OVERCOMING THE FEAR OF RUNNING OUT

No one said trusting God in the midst of challenging circumstances would always be easy. At first, when you are developing your faith, it may seem particularly difficult. However, as you grow in the Word of God, you will find yourself being able to rely on Him more easily.

So how do we overcome the fear of lack? First, let me remind you that we are not mere humans. We are people who are possessed by the Holy Spirit, which means we have the advantage over anything Satan attempts to do to contain us. We have the ability to overcome the tendency to fear lack. It doesn't matter what is going on with other people. As Christians, we stand on the Word—walking by faith, not by sight.

One of the many benefits of being a Christian is that we have a manual to refer to regarding anything we may face in life. No matter what it may be, it is covered in the Bible. Whatever the Word has to say about lack is what we are to stand on. If the Scriptures tell us we've been delivered from it, it's a done deal.

> "IF YOU ARE A BELIEVER, YOU HAVE AN UNLIMITED SOURCE OF SUPPLY."

As we approach the issue of lack, it is important to see how God has dealt with this issue in times past. First, let's take a look at Deuteronomy 2:7, which says, *"For the Lord thy God hath blessed thee in all the works of thy hand: he knoweth thy walking through this great wilderness: these forty years the LORD thy God hath been with thee; thou hast lacked nothing."* In the first part of the scripture, we see that God has already declared the work of our hands *blessed.* This means we have an empowerment to prosper available to us through our own hands. Our hands are synonymous with being instruments through which we do our work, or utilize our unique abilities. Essentially, He is saying: *I have equipped and empowered you to be successful throughout all I have called you to do.*

Second, He says that Israel walked through the wilderness for 40 years and lacked nothing! When it says they lacked nothing, it means *nothing*! All their needs were taken care of, including clothing, food, water, and their health and strength for the journey. Their feet didn't swell, their clothes didn't wear out, and they didn't run out of supplies or resources for 40 years! When it came to the basic necessities of life, they were completely sustained.

Many times, we have the wrong definition of lack. Our needs are those things that are necessary for daily living, such as food, clothing, shelter, and the things that enable us to live comfortably. Often, we put our desires in the category of needs, and then get upset when those things aren't readily accessible. However, when it comes to our needs, we will always be taken care of when we trust God. It is important that we understand the true meaning of lack.

Another scripture that demonstrates God's provision is Luke 9:3, 4. When Jesus commissioned His disciples to go out and preach the Gospel, He said, *"Take nothing for your journey, neither staves, nor scrip, neither bread, neither money; neither have two coats apiece. And whatsoever house ye enter into, there abide, and thence depart."* Can you imagine how they must have felt when they first heard Him say this? Why would Jesus tell his disciples not to take anything with them when He was about to send them on a journey? It was because He wanted to teach them how to fully trust God to meet all their needs every step of the way. The Bible says they departed and went through the towns, preaching the Gospel and healing people everywhere (v. 6). They never lacked anything at any point in time because God took care of them.

KNOWLEDGE IS POWER

The Word is full of scriptures that promise provision, all of which point to God's unconditional love for us. These promises are our guarantee that we do not have to fear lack when we trust God. First Thessalonians 4:12 says, *"That ye may walk honestly toward them that are without, and that ye may have lack of nothing."* According to this verse, it appears that being able to live a life with no lack is very possible, and it is God's will that we always have our needs met.

Psalm 34:10 confirms this further, particularly in the Amplified version, when it says, *"The young lions lack food and suffer hunger, but they who seek (inquire of and require) the Lord [by right of their need and on the authority of His Word], none of them shall lack any beneficial thing."* Would you say food and shelter are beneficial? What about clothes, transportation, and electricity? I can think of many more things that are beneficial to living a comfortable life. And God says that when we seek Him, according to His Word and in line with our needs, we will *not* lack those things!

Keep in mind that when it comes to destroying the fear of lack, it is critical that we know what God says about it. Hosea 4:6 says that God's people are destroyed because they lack knowledge. The Hebrew meaning of the word *destroyed* is "cut off." You don't have to be cut off from this tremendous provision because you lack knowledge; God's Word provides life-changing information.

Unfortunately, some people have no idea that God would even be concerned about their needs. As a result, they live their lives cut off from the provisions of God because they don't know or believe He is a provider.

With that in mind, let's look at Joshua 18:2, *"And there remained among the children of Israel seven tribes, which had not yet received their inheritance."* I don't know if you have received the inheritance God has for you, but I want to show you why these seven tribes of Israel didn't receive theirs. It can be found in Joshua 18:3, *"And Joshua said unto the children of Israel, How long are ye slack to go to possess the land, which the LORD God of your fathers hath given you?"*

The reason these Israelites didn't receive what God had for them was because they were slack. What does it mean to be slack? To be slack means to be slow to move, slow to believe, slothful, lazy, and idle. It also signifies that a person's perception is dull. When a person is slack, he or she will simply miss out on the wonderful things God has for them because their spiritual perception is cloudy. They don't recognize what belongs to them, nor do they seize it by faith.

God wants to be our source, and He wants to eliminate lack from our lives. But we cannot be slow to believe His Word. I can't begin to tell you the number of people who have failed to receive their healing or deliverance because of their lack of knowledge about God's will for their lives, which is due to a slack attitude.

Deuteronomy 28:7 says, "*The LORD shall cause thine enemies that rise up against thee to be smitten before thy face: they shall come out against thee one way, and flee before thee seven ways.*" An enemy is not always an actual person, but is simply anything that opposes us. Enemies include spiritual forces designed to contain us and keep us out of God's perfect will for our lives. Lack is a huge enemy to a person's progress. Think about it. When you have lack in some area, it affects everything from your peace to your physical well-being. There is nothing good about poverty or not having enough to handle the necessities of life.

The good news is that the Bible says God will cause our enemies to flee from before us—*seven different ways!* This means any area of lack in our lives will have to leave when it comes in contact with the burden-removing, yoke-destroying power of God. All we have to do is believe and receive it.

I encourage you to take a sheet of paper and right down every area where lack is present. Put that piece of paper in your left hand and use it as a point of contact for your faith. Now, with all the strength you have, smite that piece of paper with your right hand. Declare that those areas are made whole in the name of Jesus! Smite the spirit of lack with your faith in God's Word, and watch things begin to turn around.

Now, what I just described is not some sort of magic trick, where you hit a piece of paper with the idea that something spooky just took place. Everything comes back to the Word of God and the time we spend in His presence, developing our confidence. We must load our hearts with faith-ammunition, and fire at the areas in which lack is present by speaking those mountain-moving scriptures consistently, every day. Our faith in God's love for us is what will make the difference.

In a world marked by anxiety and the fear of dwindling resources, we have to have complete assurance that God is well able to take care of us in any economic climate. If He didn't intend to provide for us, He would never have taken care of the children of Israel those 40 years in the desert wilderness. However, since He has already done so much for those who came before us, and because He is in covenant with us through our relationship with Jesus, He is obligated to meet our needs. God never changes; He is the same yesterday, today, and forevermore. If He did it once, He will do it again.

I don't know about you, but I believe the Word. I want you to stir your faith for the impossible to take place in your life. If you don't know you've already been delivered from fear, you'll continue to operate in it. So keep the reality of God's love at the forefront of your thinking at all times. When we believe in and meditate on His unconditional love toward us, where our needs are concerned, we won't allow fear to overpower us.

Lack may be a reality in the world today, but for those who are on the Lord's side, we have absolutely nothing to worry about. Taking care of our needs is easy for God; all He needs is our faith. We have access to the unlimited, abundant resources of heaven. And when we allow the Word of God to become more real to us than our circumstances, when we seek

God and create an outflow of finances by sowing seed into the Kingdom of God, we will find ourselves living in a constant flow of provision. Have no fear; God will provide!

CHAPTER 9
Fear: An Attack on Marriage

"Charity never faileth"

(1 Corinthians 13:8).

There was a time when marriage was an institution that was honored and respected by society, families, and individuals in general. People stayed together until death, and sexual relationships outside of marriage were certainly not celebrated as normal or acceptable. However, times have changed. Gone are the days when abstinence until marriage is the norm. In fact, the trend today is for people to never marry at all, but instead, live together indefinitely. Clearly, the values of society have moved away from the standard of God's Word because selfishness has become the order of the day. Further, the enemy has unleashed an attack on marriage and relationships like never before. His objective is to inject fear into people's minds regarding marital relationships, the goal of which is to destroy the foundation of the family.

When fear is allowed to seep into our lives, it will begin to affect everything that concerns us, including our relationships. There is no such thing as having a little fear and it not eventually impact your entire life. I want to focus on marriage because it is under such attack right now. God created the institution of marriage to be the foundation of the family. His original intent was for parents to raise their children in the nurture and admonition of the Lord, so they could grow up and reproduce that prototype. Ultimately, God gets the glory when Kingdom minded people dominate the earth.

However, when Adam and Eve sinned in the Garden of Eden by disobeying God's instructions to not eat from the tree of the knowledge of good and evil, a curse entered the earth, which was driven by fear and resulted in selfishness. Jesus came to redeem mankind back to the Father and restore the family to its God-appointed position of authority; however, Satan's attack on the family has increased. He has introduced alternative lifestyles and family units that aren't God's best. Now, I know there are circumstances that take place, which force people into situations they were not prepared for, but many people have bought into the deception and have deliberately turned away from God's wisdom and abandoned His standards on purpose.

It is so awesome to know that through Jesus Christ, we have the ability to conduct our relationships the way God originally intended—governed by love and faith. We don't have to give in to the same fears the world has about marriage. As long as the Word of God is our final authority, our families can reach untold levels of success and prosperity in every area. The key is getting back to the foundation of love.

THE ATTACK ON MARRIAGE

There is no question we are living in the last days. We can be certain of this by simply looking at the Word of God and paying attention to what is going on around us in society and in the world at large. Among those who don't know God, there typically is a blatant contempt for all things godly, including traditional values and morals concerning how relationships should be conducted, specifically marriage.

There are many scriptures in the Bible that tell us how to determine the signs of the times and one of them is 1 Timothy 4:1-3, which says, *"Now the Spirit speaketh expressly, that in the latter times some shall depart from the faith, giving heed to seducing spirits, and doctrines of devils; speaking lies in hypocrisy; having their conscience seared with a hot iron; forbidding to marry..."* Even more telling is 2 Timothy 3:1-4:

> *This know also, that in the last days perilous times shall come. For men shall be lovers of their own selves, covetous, boasters, proud, blasphemers, disobedient to parents, unthankful, unholy, without natural affection, trucebreakers, false accusers, incontinent, fierce, despisers of those that are good, traitors, heady, highminded, lovers of pleasures more than lovers of God...*

Notice the first characteristic the Apostle Paul says will describe the attitudes of people in the last days—that they would be *lovers of their own selves*. It also says that they would be lovers of pleasures more than lovers of God. Selfishness, which is fear based, is the primary theme in the world system. It has become the norm in people's lives and is evident in the way people approach marriage, from the sanctioning of homosexual marriages to "shacking up." Fear breeds selfishness, which *always* causes us to turn our backs on God's Word.

COHABITATION: A FEAR-BASED ALTERNATIVE TO THE REAL THING

Did you know the number of never-married men and women rose from 21 million in 1970 to 52 million by 2005? The reason has a lot to do with a rising trend among dating and engaged couples called cohabitation. Every year, millions of men and women choose to move in together as an alternative to fully committing to the marriage covenant. There are all kinds of reasons people use to justify why living together before marriage is the way to go. Some argue that it is the best way to "test the relationship" or see if they are "compatible" with a potential mate, and some say it is for financial reasons. Others come from broken homes themselves and are afraid of divorce, so they convince themselves that living together will somehow equip them with the knowledge they need to be successful in a marriage with their significant other.

What these men and women fail to realize is that living together is a counterfeit of marriage. It dishonors God and the individuals' relationship with each other. It is based in selfishness and fear, not real love. In addition, it actually sabotages any real chance at having a healthy marriage. Statistics reveal that cohabiting couples who eventually tie the knot have a much higher rate of divorce. However, the majority of these couples never get married.

Cohabitation is the key reason why the number of people getting married is steadily declining, and it is also a reason why many marriages are *failing*. It is a direct attack on the institution of marriage. Studies show that half of cohabiting relationships end within fifteen months—without a wedding. When we enter into a relationship with self-preservation on our minds, there is no way we can truly have a healthy relationship. Real, authentic love doesn't take advantage of others; it gives the advantage. When a man and woman choose to "try each other out" they actually initiate

> "GOD INTENDED FOR US TO STAY MARRIED FOREVER."

a performance-based relationship that is full of conditions and fear. "If you do this for me, the way I like, I might do this for you." Living together is really based in a fear of commitment and a fear of divorce, and we know that when fear is present, it will connect us to the things we are afraid of.

The enemy hates marriage because it was designed to be the platform from which godly children would be produced. The last thing Satan wants is more god-fearing people to dominate the earth. So he uses the fear and hurt people have in their lives to convince them of an alternative way of relating to one another. He wants to get people so far off track from God's way of doing things that they never reach or experience the good life the Father originally intended. When we give in to our fears and choose to follow our own plans rather than God's plan, we set ourselves up for failure.

Contrary to the picture the world paints of marriage being a ball and chain, or some sort of miserable shackle, it is actually a wonderful thing! However, it requires a full commitment going in. Love is more than a feeling; it is a decision to love another person through the best and worst of times, unconditionally. With the right person, done the right way, it can be like heaven on earth! The key is to allow the God-kind of love, not fear-based selfishness, to be the foundation of our relationships with one another. When we trust God and operate our relationships according to His Word, divorce will never be a consideration, and our marriages will succeed.

DIVORCE: WHEN SELFISHNESS GAINS THE UPPER HAND

It seems divorces are on the rise now more than ever before, and sadly, Christian couples are leading the way. As a pastor, I cannot tell you the number of ministers and preachers I have counseled or spoken to regarding their decision to divorce their mates. As members of the body of Christ, this should not be. God intended for us to stay married forever.

The issue of divorce in the Church is a touchy one because people have heard so many different things about what is and is not sanctioned by the Word of God. The Bible does give a specific condition under which divorce is an option—sexual sin outside the marriage. Matthew 5:32 says that fornication is a viable reason for divorce. This is because when adultery enters the picture, the marriage covenant is severed. This means that both spouses are in the same position they were before they were married, in that they are now single from a spiritual perspective. The spouse who was cheated on now has the choice of whether he or she wants to start all over.

While there are many couples who do choose to stay together and work out their marriages despite an adulterous affair, it is not required by the Word in this situation. In a fornication scenario, the couple is free to divorce and should not feel guilty or condemned about that decision. I also believe that if a spouse is in a physically abusive situation where his or her life is in danger, it is in his or her best interest to get out of the relationship.

Unfortunately, too many people are divorcing for reasons that really can and should be worked out according to the Word. Things like, "I'm not happy anymore" and "I'm no longer in love with my spouse" are not reasons to end a marriage. These types of issues boil down to one thing—selfishness.

Every married person has gone through challenges, difficult moments, and times when he or she did not *feel* like they were in love. However, the love that holds a marriage together is not based on feelings; it is based on commitment. We must make the decision ahead of time to remain faithful to our covenant, no matter how we feel.

So where does fear come in? Fear is the foundation for selfishness, which is what drives most people to leave their marriages. When we are in fear, we will try to preserve the part of ourselves we really need to change.

For example, I don't particularly care for going to shopping malls. Taffi, on the other hand, could do it all day! There was a time when she would ask me to go with her, and I would be in a miserable mood through the whole experience. I may have had a fear that this would become a regular thing, or that I was somehow going to be pressured into doing something I really didn't like doing, so I maintained a negative attitude about it to protect my stance. One day I realized I needed to make an adjustment in the way I was looking at things. Instead of only considering *my* feelings about shopping, I made a conscious effort to consider Taffi. This is what unconditional love is all about—putting someone else's needs and desires above your own. When I changed my attitude, the shopping outings ceased to be burdensome. I learned how to enjoy hanging out with my wife while doing something she loved.

I know this was a simple example, but the foundational principle is what we need to be focusing on. If marriages are going to work, both people must choose the love route. I have heard husbands say they just don't feel like they are in love with they're wives anymore, and I can only respond by saying, it's not about how you feel. Marriages go through seasons, and some seasons may not feel like the honeymoon phase. However, it is during those times that we must do loving things on purpose, and look for ways to move beyond our own selfish feelings. If we start to bless our spouses, as an act of our will, by faith, it won't be long before our feelings will line up. The Holy Spirit can rekindle the marital flame if we will yield to Him and give Him the opportunity to so do.

Divorce is not the answer to temporary feelings of discontentment. Every argument and issue that comes up in a marriage forces us to choose one of two things—love or selfishness. We must always ask ourselves if our choices and responses are coming from a place of unconditional love or self-preservation. Our responsibility as Believers is to choose love every time. If we do, we are guaranteed to make the right decision.

DON'T RUN FROM YOUR DEVELOPMENT

Marriage is the ultimate journey toward spiritual and character development, which is why we cannot run away from it when things get uncomfortable. All the tests and trials we experience in our relationships with our spouses are designed to make us better and stronger. How can we ever mature in the love of God if we turn our backs on the process?

You may be wondering how to develop in the love of God from a practical standpoint. Well, my answer isn't "deep" or overly spiritual. It all boils down to a decision. In our interactions with our spouses, every day, we must determine whether we will choose to speak and act out of a place of love or selfishness. In a marriage relationship, we will have plenty of opportunities to do this.

For example, a husband may feel as if his wife isn't meeting one of his core needs for respect, or a wife may feel her need for affection isn't being met. These are common issues in marriages. Many times, husbands and wives do not know or understand exactly what the other's core needs are as a man or woman and the result is a lot of frustration. On top of that, miscommunication can make the situation worse.

In a situation like this, both people must be willing to choose the love route in how they deal with the other person. Often, the problem comes in when neither person wants to adjust his or her behavior because of selfishness. However, this is still not a reason to abandon the marriage. Spouses want to point the finger at each other instead of accepting their roles in the problem; it always takes two to tango. The key is to understand that even if the other person does not immediately change, the commitment to walk in love must remain the same. This means that even if a man goes to his wife and says, "Honey, I don't feel respected by you because of A, B, C, and D, let's discuss how to change this," his decision to walk in love toward her cannot be determined by whether she responds positively to his request. The same is true for the wife who has an issue with her husband.

Unconditional love is just that—unconditional.

First Corinthians 13:8 says that love *never* fails. That means that we can never apply love to any situation and not ultimately see change take place in that circumstance. Too many people run out on their marriages before allowing the restorative, healing process of love to run its course. If they will only stay where they were, they will see transformation take place in their lives as well as in the lives of their spouses. The love of God is the gateway to His power, and that power will never stop working once it is in operation.

It is usually our fears and insecurities that keep us from completely submitting to the love of God. We become afraid that if we walk in love, we will be taken advantage of by the other person. Many women fear submitting to their husbands because they think it means giving up their freedom, or that it will give their husbands license to be controlling. Husbands fear completely walking in love toward their wives for some of the same reasons. As you can see, fear has the potential to absolutely destroy any relationship. We don't want our egos to be bruised, so we hide behind our fear instead of allowing ourselves to be vulnerable. But when we make love our lifestyle, it eradicates fear and guarantees a favorable outcome.

I know of wives who had difficult husbands, and through their choice to walk in love toward them, those men changed for the better. The same thing can happen with a man whose wife has issues as well; it makes no difference. When love is applied, it will never fail, ever. The choice is yours.

Marriage statistics don't have to paint a negative picture when we allow love, and not selfishness, to be the predominant force in our lives. I look forward to the day when the statistics of Christians staying together overshadow the ones highlighting the divorce rates! If you are single, there is no need to stress out about getting married or try to rush the process; God wants you to enjoy your season of being single and the development you experience during that time is invaluable. However, marriage is nothing to run from either. Don't be afraid of it.

The world would like to portray the institution of marriage in a negative light, even convincing people that they shouldn't bother with it at all, but these ideas are fear-based and selfish. God doesn't want us to be alone because He wants us to develop in love. Being in a committed relationship with a lifelong partner provides the perfect opportunity for this type of growth. Don't allow fear to cause you to throw the towel in on something God intended to be a blessing to you. Embrace the standard of God's Word as your final authority rather than the world's way, and begin to experience new levels of success in your relationships, from start to finish.

CHAPTER 10
Is Lust Fear-Based?

"But the fruit of the Spirit is love, joy, peace, longsuffering, gentle-
ness, goodness, faith, meekness, temperance: against such there is
no law. And they that are Christ's have crucified the
flesh with the affections and lusts"
(Galatians 5:19-21).

One of the objectives of this book is to expose the many
faces of fear and provide answers to eliminating this destructive
force altogether. There are so many roads that fear can lead us
down, and many times we don't realize that most of the negative
behavior people engage in is really fear-based. If we can get to
the root of the issue, and eliminate the source, we take a major
step in living free from the bondage that is tied to it. It may be
surprising, but lust is fear-driven and fear-based. It is one of
those areas that keep people trapped in destructive habits and
addictions for a very long time. The basic anatomy of lust is a
seed that is introduced to the mind and allowed to grow. When
lust is in operation, you can be certain that fear is present.

At the root of every work of the flesh listed in Galatians 5:19-21 is fear, which is supported by selfishness. This passage of scripture describes what the works of the flesh are: *"Now the works of the flesh are manifest, which are these; adultery, fornication, uncleanness, lasciviousness, idolatry, witchcraft, hatred, variance, emulations, wrath, strife, seditions, heresies, envyings, murders, drunkenness, revellings, and such like..."* I specifically want to focus on lust because lust is at the root of many of the works of the flesh, and it is something so many people struggle with on a daily basis.

Lust, which is an intense appetite for something, is an ignition switch that turns on so many destructive things. We commonly think of lust in terms of sexual sin, which is accurate, but it can also apply to anything we begin to desire with intensity, to the point where it drives us to act out in ways that go against God's Word. Lust can be present in the area of eating, which leads to gluttony, and it can even cause people to become so hungry for power that they will do anything for a position of influence. When lust completely takes over a person's life, he or she enters into *lasciviousness*, which means having no restraint.

Perhaps you are wondering where fear comes into play in all of this. Actually, the fear the enemy uses to entice people to lust is the fear that they will miss out on something by not going after what their flesh wants. To begin to get an understanding, let's take a look at lust and how it works in a person's mind and heart.

James 1:14 says, *"But every man is tempted, when he is drawn away of his own lust, and enticed."* The first thing we see in this scripture is that temptation is able to draw away the person who already has lust in his or her heart. Everyone will be tempted, but everyone will *not* be "drawn away." The determining factor lies in what is already present in our hearts.

So we now see that lust is something that resides in the heart, or the spirit of a man. And it gets there through the three gates—the eyes (what we look at), the ears (what we listen to), and the mouth (what we talk about). What we look at, listen to, and talk about in abundance will eventually overwhelm and overtake our lives. If we meditate on images, words, and ideas that go against God's Word and feed our carnal appetites, the enemy will have no problem drawing us away with a particular temptation. When we lust for something, we essentially allow ourselves to be distracted by that desire. It begins with a thought and progresses to a mindset and ultimately takes action. When a particular lust is turned on in a person's life, the enemy uses fear to keep it going.

For example, in the area of sexual lust, say a man is in line at the grocery store, and he notices an attractive woman in front of him who is very visually appealing. The enemy will naturally inject a thought in his mind, telling him to take a second and third look at the woman. If the man follows through on that suggestion and doesn't choose to look away as an act of his will, an image of that particular woman will be implanted in his mind, and he will begin to desire her in an inappropriate way. If this man doesn't have any knowledge of how to cast down thoughts, the lustful seed that was planted in his mind will begin to grow, and it won't be long before he will begin seeking out ways to fulfill that desire, whether physically or visually.

Once that lustful cycle has been activated, Satan will use fear to keep it going. That feeling of potentially missing out on the next thrill or encounter will be in operation again, and will convince the person that he or she *must* ride the desire out into actual manifestation. There is the sense that if they don't act on what they are feeling, they won't make it. Clearly, fear is the driving factor behind lustful behavior.

Did you know there are men whose goal in life is to sleep with as many women as possible? They can't even see an attractive woman without lusting after her and pursuing the fulfillment of their selfish desires. The thought process is, *If I don't pursue her, she may get away.* There is the constant fear of missing out on an experience that the enemy convinces them is a necessity at the moment. Unfortunately, the attempt to fulfill lust only results in disappointment and disillusionment because it can never be satisfied. Every encounter ends up leaving a person wanting more but never fulfilled. Even worse is being trapped in a cycle of lustful behavior without the ability to find the brakes.

Another area where lust enters and fear drives the behavior is food. On a more intense level, lustful appetites for food can lead to things like morbid obesity and other serious health problems. People who eat beyond their bodies' natural capacities are usually trying to fill some sort of void, and food becomes a source of comfort to them. Some even fear losing weight because they identify the weight with the security they feel the extra pounds provide.

On a smaller scale, I think all of us have encountered moments of lust where our eating habits are concerned. Think about how many times we have eaten more than we should have at an event, or overindulged in our favorite treat. We may have loaded our plates up or "overdosed" on a particular dessert only to find ourselves feeling sick afterwards! I can definitely relate to this because I had a problem with lasciviousness when it came to apple pies, which happen to be my favorite dessert. There was a time in my life when I would eat an entire pie in one sitting, and it wasn't because I was hungry. I would eat until I felt the sugar in my system, and it was affecting my health. I had a lust for apple pie!

This may sound humorous, but in those moments, if we really think about it, there is a fear there that we might not get a chance to eat this particular meal or food again, or that someone else might take the last of whatever it is we want at the moment. The behavior is completely fear-based! It isn't about the natural desire for food in those moments; it's about getting all we can before there is none left for us. The fear of running out is at the root of the behavior.

Lust is futile because it can never be satisfied. Many people have allowed their minds to become blinded by the enemy's deception where their desires are concerned, and they are trapped in their behavior. A life that is governed by lust is an empty one. The fear of missing out will actually rob us of the great things God has designed for our lives; things He wants to give us through His Word and by doing things His way. The enemy tries to convince us that by fulfilling our selfish desires, they will be quenched. He tells us that we will still be in control of the situation; however, our carnal desires will continue to trouble us until we submit them to God's Word. The fear that drives the behavior is only fed by acting out on the lust; it doesn't go away. Until the fear is dealt with, the lust will always be present.

GOD HAS A BETTER WAY

One of the things that make lust such a driving force is the sense of urgency that accompanies it. It is the feeling of having to immediately gratify ourselves. The fulfillment that lust seeks to obtain is really a counterfeit for what God wants to do in our lives. He has a better way of reaching the goal of being satisfied in life, and He doesn't want us to allow selfishness to be what drives us.

Every promise in the Bible is designed to bring lasting satisfaction in life. Unlike what the devil has to offer, God's fulfillment is not the elusive kind that always seems just out of reach. He really does provide everything we need if we can only trust Him with every aspect of our lives. When we understand and know the love God has for us, we won't settle for the counterfeit of lust.

In my years of counseling, I have discovered that people who habitually engage in addictive, self-destructive behavior that involves lust are really empty on the inside. Often, they are the ones who are longing for acceptance and love, and are actually searching for these things through outside sources, whether it is through sexual encounters or comfort food.

When we operate in lust, there is also another fear at work in us—the fear that there is no real benefit in doing things God's way. For example, a person who has given themselves over to a spirit of lust where sex is concerned actually fears giving up their behavior because they perceive God's way of doing things as a burden. It may seem unfathomable to a man or woman who has been having sex outside of marriage to change his or her behavior and remain abstinent until marriage because they don't see or understand the value in it. The world system tells us we have to "try things out" to see if we are compatible with one another in a relationship. When we believe these lies long enough, it can actually breed a fear of obeying God.

I want to make something clear—*anything* God instructs us to do has a tremendous benefit and blessing attached to it. His guidelines are not designed to make life miserable, but are there to actually enhance the quality of our lives overall. When we submit to the fear of losing out rather than faith in what God has to offer us through His Word, we put ourselves at the mercy of our flesh. Choosing our way of doing things over God's way will not take us down the right path because it is always going to be based in fear and selfishness.

Psalm 16:11 says something so powerful, *"Thou wilt shew me the path of life: in thy presence is fulness of joy; at thy right hand there are pleasures for evermore."* Most people don't make a connection between God and pleasure, but the Bible says there are everlasting pleasures available to us through Him. That's good news for people struggling with lust because it lets us know that the pleasure God has to offer will never end. God will never give us unquenchable desires that can never be fulfilled or that are based on the fear of missing out on something. The pleasures God makes available to us are richly satisfying in every way.

Lust is a direct attack on the provision of God because it tells us a lie. Anytime we try to obtain something outside of God's will, we are headed for trouble. Sex with people we are not married to only creates a web of soul ties, broken emotions, unhealthy expectations, and even physical complications. When we lust after anything, we are open to all kinds of suggestions from the enemy about how to go about getting it, and none of them are based on the love of God. Our heavenly Father has a better way of doing things—a way that will not cost us our peace and well-being.

The Bible is full of promises from God, but one of the key passages of scripture that describes how we are to go about obtaining the things we desire is Matthew 6:33, which says, *"But seek ye first the kingdom of God, and his righteousness; and all these things shall be added unto you."* This scripture is activated through faith, not fear. The preceding scriptures talk about provision, such as food and clothing, and how those who don't know God seek after these things as their first priority. I also think those scriptures can apply to seeking after the fulfillment of things through lust and selfish desire instead of trusting God. When we seek God's way of doing things, which is outlined in His Word, we won't look for fulfillment through sexual encounters outside of marriage, or anything else for that matter. Seeking God's way of doing things means putting His Word first in our lives and allowing our love for Him to drive out the fears that are behind our selfishness and lust. In God are the relationships, success, health, wealth, and peace we seek. In Him we become whole so that we do not look to things outside of our relationship with God to fulfill us.

GETTING LUST OUT OF OUR LIVES

Since lust is fear-based and selfish, the answer to getting rid of it is to become immersed in the love of God. God is love, and perfect love casts out fear. Developing in the love of God is the proper way to effectively deal with lust, along with renewing our minds by reading God's Word.

Galatians 5:19, 21 describe the works of the flesh and also tells us that those who operate in these things will not inherit the benefits of God's Word. However, He doesn't abandon us to our lustful desires without giving us the answer to how to deal with them. In the scriptures immediately following, He says, *"But the fruit of the Spirit is love, joy, peace, longsuffering, gentleness, goodness, faith, meekness, temperance: against such there is no law. And they that are Christ's have crucified the flesh with the affections and lusts"* (vv. 22, 23). Love is the fruit of the Spirit, and each characteristic of love is described in this passage. When it comes to dealing with any work of the flesh, one of these characteristics of God's personality must be exercised and developed.

Lust is selfish, and selfishness is attached to fear. Since that is the case, it makes sense that exercising temperance, an aspect of love, is the answer to overcoming lust. When we trust God and His love for us, we are essentially walking in the love of God. And the Bible says there is no law that has the power to overcome this love. This means that not even Satan and the law of sin and death can conquer a person who has made a quality decision to walk in the love of God, no matter how they feel, or what their flesh wants.

It is the Holy Spirit's job to support and help us walk out our Christian life. He empowers us to be strong when we are confronted with desires that do not line up with the Word. God never said that wrong thoughts wouldn't crop up and try to gain the upperhand in our lives; how we handle them is the key.

> "SINCE LUST IS FEAR-BASED AND SELFISH, THE ANSWER TO GETTING RID OF IT IS TO BECOME IMMERSED IN THE LOVE OF GOD."

Romans 12:1, 2 talks about the importance of renewing our minds so we are not conformed to the world's way of doing things. If the world says it is okay to go after whatever our flesh wants, the Word will say the exact opposite. What will we choose to obey—our flesh or the Bible? Our choices are reflected in the degree to which our minds have been renewed in a particular area. The only way to do that is to meditate and practice the Word of God until our thinking changes.

Meditating on God's love for us, as well as wanting to please the Father out of our love for Him, will help us develop a love-consciousness that conquers any fear-based lust we may have in our hearts. We will begin to see that we don't have to compromise or give in to what our flesh wants in the moment, out of fear that we are missing out on something. God offers so much more than Satan does. The more time we spend in His Word, the more we will realize that He has a perfect plan for our lives that includes a wealth of blessings and unlimited pleasure in every area of our lives. When we make His Word our final authority, He will begin to reveal Himself to us in an unprecedented way, and He will empower us to overcome the spirit of lust. Love always wins over fear and selfishness. Which one will you choose? I urge you to choose love.

CHAPTER 11
Combating Fear of the End Times

"...see that ye be not troubled: for all these things must come to pass, but the end is not yet"

(Matthew 24:6).

As we draw closer to the return of the Lord Jesus Christ, one thing is for certain—fear is at an all-time high and will continue to rise among those in the world who do not know Him. In fact, the Bible says that in the last days men's hearts would fail them because of fear. For those who do not know Jesus Christ, the future is uncertain. There are those who sense bad things on the horizon and others who think all is well. Thankfully, Believers have the Word of God to rely on as their guide during these turbulent times in which we live. Jesus has already forewarned us of what is to come, and God's Word gives us the security we need for the days ahead. When we put our faith in the Scriptures, we will not fear the future.

Have you noticed a marked increase in the frequency and intensity of not only natural disasters, which seem to be taking place on nearly a bi-weekly basis, but of violence, perversion, and general lawlessness on a national and global scale? If you have not made the connection between the end of the world as we know it and the increase in such occurrences, it is time to wake up and smell the coffee. Satan has launched an all-out attack on everything pertaining to God, and is unleashing demonic activity in the earth like never before. It is his last-ditch effort to deceive as many people as possible before Jesus returns. Even the earth is reeling under the spiritual weight of sin that is rampant nowadays.

While the news reports are growing more appalling on a daily basis, these things should not come as a surprise to Christians. There are plenty of scriptures which specifically point out such occurrences in detail. The fact that God has prepared us ahead of time is a great relief, and it shows His love for us. He hasn't left us in the dark; we are not at the mercy of Satan's attacks.

Matthew 24 is a powerful chapter because in it Jesus describes to the disciples what the signs of His coming would be, as well as what to expect in the last days. I find it fascinating that thousands of years prior to this time we are living in, these men questioned Jesus about the very things we are seeing now! Even then, there must have been fear and uncertainty about the future. However, Jesus clearly outlined *exactly* what the signs of His return would be. His words resonate with truth and clarity today, just as they did then. Matthew 24:3-13 says:

And as he sat upon the mount of Olives, the disciples came unto him privately, saying, Tell us, when shall these things be? and what shall be the sign of thy coming, and of the end of the world? And Jesus answered and said unto them, Take heed that no man deceive you. For many shall come in my name, saying, I am Christ; and shall deceive many. And ye shall hear of wars and rumours of wars: see that ye be not troubled: for all these things must come to pass, but the end is not yet. For nation shall rise against nation, and kingdom against kingdom: and there shall be famines, and pestilences, and earthquakes, in divers places. All these are the beginning of sorrows. Then shall they deliver you up to be afflicted, and shall kill you: and ye shall be hated of all nations for my name's sake. And then shall many be offended, and shall betray one another, and shall hate one another. And many false prophets shall rise, and shall deceive many. And because iniquity shall abound, the love of many shall wax cold. But he that shall endure unto the end, the same shall be saved.

I love the Lord because He never allows us to go into any situation blindly. I think if we allow this chapter to be the lens through which we view the end times it will set our minds at ease in many ways.

In this passage of scripture, Jesus describes several things that we are seeing now, the first of which is deception. The fact that the Lord warned us not to allow anyone to deceive us means that deception would be the norm in the last days, and He knew it. We see this today all the time. There are all kinds of views and teachings about God and life that are being accepted but aren't in alignment with the Word of God. We can avoid being deceived by allowing the Word to be the final authority in *every* area of our lives. Because the Word is our standard, we don't have to be afraid of being deceived. That means if we hear someone saying they represent Jesus, but what they are preaching or teaching doesn't line up with the Bible, we immediately know to discard it. When we are faced with the norms and values of society that clearly contradict what the Word says, we won't be deceived into thinking those things are somehow okay. Getting the Word in our hearts in abundance and *abiding* in it keeps us well-protected from the enemy.

The second thing Jesus mentions is wars and rumors of wars. I don't know about you, but I believe this is definitely becoming the norm. Countries seem to be gearing up for confrontation, particularly where nuclear warfare is concerned. The nation of Israel and the surrounding area is a particular hotbed of spiritual and physical conflict. Jesus says to *"be not troubled: for these things must come to pass, but the end is not yet."* Once again, He offers words of encouragement to quell any fear we may have about what will happen next.

The next three things Jesus describes after His discussion about nations and kingdoms rising up against each other are famines, pestilences, and earthquakes in diverse places. I think these are probably most obvious and get the most prevalent media attention because they are happening so regularly. Earthquakes and other natural disasters are literally taking place almost weekly. New and more potent strains of disease are being discovered, and countries all over the world are suffering from severe famine and poverty. Never before have we seen these things taking place with such frequency and intensity. We shouldn't be frightened, however, because these occurrences are simply signaling the return of the Lord! If anything, it is cause for Believers everywhere to start rejoicing and taking inventory of their lives with more scrutiny.

The final part of this passage deals with the attitudes and mindsets that people in the world will have in the last days, not only toward Christians and the things of God, but in general. Jesus describes an intense hatred for Believers, as well as offense, betrayal, iniquity, and hardened hearts that are devoid of God's love. I think we can see evidence of these things on a regular basis. The world hates God and anything having to do with Christianity. The name of Jesus is the only name that

> "YOU CAN HAVE FAITH FOR THE FUTURE BY CHOOSING GOD'S WORD AND HIS LOVE OVER ANYTHING ELSE THAT MAY VIE FOR YOUR ATTENTION."

incites people to anger and defensiveness. People's hearts are hardened against the truth and what is wrong is viewed as right! Satan is doing everything He can to remove the mere mention of God from day-to-day life. This is the reality of the world in which we live.

Second Timothy 3:1-7 also mentions the behavior that would be prevalent during this time. When we see people hurting others, acting out on their lust, and engaging in behavior that is selfish and destructive, we should not be fearful, intimidated, or shocked. Instead, we should do everything we can do demonstrate God's love and character in spite of what we see other people doing. When we represent the Kingdom of God in the midst of ungodliness, we are able to make an impact in the lives of others.

THE TRUTH ABOUT THE RAPTURE

The catching away of the Body of Christ, also known as the Rapture, is a significant end-time event, which, for many Believers, is shrouded in mystery and uncertainty. Many Christians are unaware of exactly what the Rapture is and what it signifies. Others have heard about it, but do not keep it at the forefront of their thinking on a daily basis. There are many different levels of understanding and faith in the body of Christ; however, I believe now, more than ever, is the time to talk about the Rapture so that fear doesn't have an opportunity to creep in.

Keep in mind that whenever we are uncertain or in the dark about something, fear is most likely present. Think about the concept of being afraid of the dark. The reason is because you can't see what is in front of you. There is the feeling that something may be present in the room that you are unaware of. However, when you flip the light switch, the fear is dispelled because you can now see what is in your immediate surroundings.

The same is true when it comes to future events in the last days. Hosea 4:6 says God's people perish because of a lack of knowledge. What we don't know *can* hurt us. Not being enlightened on a particular subject can be the gateway for fear to come on the scene and destroy our faith.

First Thessalonians 4:16-18 says this:

> For the Lord himself shall descend from heaven with a shout, with the voice of the archangel, and with the trump of God: and the dead in Christ shall rise first: Then we which are alive and remain shall be caught up together with them in the clouds, to meet the Lord in the air: and so shall we ever be with the Lord. Wherefore comfort one another with these words.

The word "rapture" is not specifically used to reference this phenomenal event that is going to take place; however, rapture means "caught up," which the Bible does make reference to in this passage of Scripture. The Rapture is essentially the catching away of the Church of Jesus Christ. It is the removal of true Christians from the earth prior to the release of God's judgment on those who continue to reject Him. The Rapture is going to usher in a

7-year period of time known as the Tribulation, during which the Antichrist will be revealed and begin his attempt at world domination. The Tribulation will be the most devastating time period the world has ever seen or known, and it will also be a time of unprecedented persecution of Christians and Jewish people.

The Rapture is an aspect of the return of the Lord but differs from the Second Coming of the Lord, which is an event that will be evident and apparent to *all* people on the earth. The Rapture is something that only those who are truly a part of the Body of Christ will be aware of and experience. These are two completely separate occurrences.

The idea of millions of Christians being air-lifted out of the earth into heaven probably seems far-fetched to those who are more focused on the physical realm than the heavenly realm; however, God's Word is true. This event *is* going to take place and it will be devastating to those who are left behind. The good news is that God has once again given us the forewarning we need to prepare for His trumpet call.

If we stay ready for the Rapture, we won't have to fear the event itself because we will *be* ready when it takes place. First Thessalonians 5:2-9 (*The Amplified Bible*) gives us some wonderful insight and instruction to remain in a position of readiness at all times. We do not have to fear missing this glorious event. We are the righteousness of God by faith in Christ, seated with Him in heavenly places. The Apostle Paul is writing to the church at Thessalonica here and he says:

For you yourselves know perfectly well that the day of the [return of the] Lord will come [as unexpectedly and suddenly] as a thief in the night. When people are saying, All is well and secure, and, There is peace and safety, then in a moment unforeseen destruction (ruin and death) will come upon them as suddenly as labor pains come upon a woman with child; and they shall by no means escape, for there will be no escape. But you are not in [given up to the power of] darkness, brethren, for that day to overtake you by surprise like a thief. For you are all sons of light and sons of the day; we do not belong either to the night or to darkness. Accordingly then, let us not sleep, as the rest do, but let us keep wide awake (alert, watchful, cautious, and on our guard) and let us be sober (calm, collected, and circumspect)...For God has not appointed us to [incur His] wrath [He did not select us to condemn us], but [that we might] obtain [His] salvation through our Lord Jesus Christ (the Messiah).

First, Paul says the Rapture will take place like a thief in the night, which lets us know it will happen unexpectedly. For the person, however, who is aware of this future event, they will not be caught off guard. He also lets us know that it will happen when most people think everything is secure and stable. There are a lot of folks who think things in the world are okay for the most part and that they will get better. However, those who know the Word of God know that conditions in the world will only get worse as time goes on, which is why we put our trust in God. Sometimes it is easier to convince ourselves that all is well than to actually deal with the reality that the opposite is true and we need to make some changes. Paul says that just when people begin to get comfortable with the current state of things, the catching away of the Church will take place, and there will be no escape from the disaster that will follow.

Besides describing the Rapture itself, Paul also tells Believers how to prepare for it by making sure they are walking and living in the light of God and not in darkness. He says those who are not children of darkness will not be surprised by the Rapture. How do we know if we are children of the light? By accepting Jesus as our Lord and Savior and receiving our righteousness by faith in the blood of Jesus, we become light in darkness. The Word brings light into dark areas, and when it is transforming our thinking and behavior, we are in tune with the Spirit of God. We will be sensitive to His voice and will hear the Lord when He calls us. As Believers, we are to be on guard and "sober," meaning we should never allow our thinking to be intoxicated by the ideas and values of this current world system, which is deception. God fully intends to spare Believers from the tribulation that is coming on this world.

THE BEST WAY TO PREPARE

I often say that when Jesus calls the Church to heaven in

the Rapture, He is going to be looking for those who have a relationship with Him and who look like Him. What does Jesus look like? The answer to this question can be summed up in one word—*love*. The best way we can prepare ourselves for end-time events is by developing in the love of God. Not only will love allow us to represent Jesus in an ungodly world, but it will also drive fear out of our hearts. Walking in love is guaranteed to be the most effective way to ensure we please the Lord in these last days.

Love is the cornerstone of everything God does, including the execution of His end-time plans. There are a lot of wonderful things in store for those who trust and believe in Him. Even during the Tribulation, God's love will continue to be at work in the earth, drawing people to Him so their souls may be saved. Right now, our goal must be to demonstrate God's character in everything we do so that we can eliminate selfishness. First John 4:16 says that God *is* love, and the person who dwells, or lives, in the love life matures spiritually. In addition, perfected love casts out fear.

Understanding this, it becomes clear that in order to eliminate fear of what is going to happen in the last days we *must* make walking in love our priority. Love has a protective effect, and it actually shields us from the enemy. The Bible says it never fails, so you can never go wrong by developing in it. It is God's very nature and character, which is why every force of the enemy is powerless against it.

First Corinthians 13 must be the cornerstone of our

Christian life because it describes what love really is. If we will focus on growing into the true definition of love, we will find ourselves developing in the image of Christ, and fear will be cast out. We will know for certain that Jesus will recognize us when He calls us to Him. *"Herein is love, not that we loved God, but that he loved us, and sent his Son to be the propitiation for our sins"* (1 John 4:10).

Every day we will have opportunities to develop patience, kindness, humility, and meekness, and to shun rudeness, meanness, jealousy, and pride. Each time we choose the love route instead of selfishness, we practice the love of God. This is how we become God-conscious during turbulent times. The result is absolute confidence in the preeminent power of God's love for us, and access to the power of God itself. And with a mindset that is love-focused, the end-times become the most significant and exciting time in the history of the world—a time during which we have the opportunity to bring more people into the kingdom of God than ever before.

You can have faith for the future by choosing God's Word and His love over anything else that may vie for your attention. There will be many distractions designed to get you off course and minimize the reality of what is going to happen in the days ahead, but remain steadfast in your commitment to the truth. You have nothing to fear with God's love dwelling in you and manifesting through you. The Holy Spirit will lead and guide you every step of the way. Rejoice, because, in God, your future is bright!

CHAPTER 12
Overcoming the Fear of Abandonment

"Let your conversation be without covetousness; and be content with such things as ye have: for he hath said, I will never leave thee, nor forsake thee"

(Hebrews 13:5).

Have you ever experienced a time in your life when you felt as if God had left you? Perhaps you experienced abandonment at an early age, and it impacted you well into your adult life. Many times, our personal experiences from childhood, as well as those in our adult years, can cause us to have a fear of abandonment—especially where relationships are concerned. There are many people who feel they can never fully entrust their hearts to others because they feel, deep down, that they ultimately will find themselves all alone. Sometimes this fear even causes people to sabotage their relationships to avoid getting hurt again. Overcoming the fear of abandonment is not easy, but by understanding and accepting the truth that God loves us, we can grow to new levels of trust and acceptance in our relationships with others.

Every human being has four basic needs. They are acceptance, identity, security, and purpose. Our heavenly Father wants to use the right relationships to meet these four needs in our lives. However, the problem is, many times people are unfulfilled in one or more of these four areas, and it causes a deficiency in their souls—which affects the way they relate to others. Past hurts and disappointments can open the door to the fear of that pain getting worse or being compounded if they allow themselves to get close to another person.

I want to examine these four areas so we can make the connection between the fear of abandonment and unmet needs. The first is the need for acceptance. What do I mean by *acceptance*? I'm talking about knowing you are loved and needed by others. Everyone needs to feel accepted on this core level. Even people who say, "Well, I don't need anybody" crave acceptance. They don't really believe they don't need others. It's just that they are hurt or angry, and self-preservation has kicked in. Hurt people always see things through a warped lens, and end up making decisions that support their fear and hurt.

Knowing we are loved and accepted is vital to our ability to trust others and have healthy relationships in the future. Ideally, this need should be fulfilled as we are being raised by our parents, but unfortunately, different situations take place through which Satan interferes with the proper development of acceptance. Many times this happens through the breakup of the family unit through divorce, separation, or other issues going on in the household. The enemy knows if he can destroy the family, the children will come out of the situation unfulfilled in some of the most basic areas. When children feel abandoned by their parents, either physically or emotionally, that issue will carry over into their adult experience.

You may know someone who has an intense need to be loved and accepted, sometimes to the point where he or she engages in unbecoming behavior or gets involved in unhealthy relationships. Sometimes people do these things unknowingly, not realizing that the reason they make the choices they do is because they are looking for acceptance by any means necessary. God wants us to know that we are accepted unconditionally by Him, and He loves us. As we develop in our relationship with Him, we will see that nothing we do or don't do can separate us from His love (Romans 8:35, 39).

The second basic need every person has is the need for identity. Having a sense of identity means that we know we are significant and special individuals. Again, this is something that should be imparted from parents to their children. When a child is the victim of a broken home or a dysfunctional family, a real identity crisis takes place. The child usually does not have a healthy identity, which can sometimes lead to emotional problems. The same is true for people who don't know who they are as a child of God. They are open to other voices from the world, which go against God's Word. Women who are in search of that feeling of identity (and security) may choose men who appear to fill that void, but they are actually the worst possible choices for a mate. The same is true for men. When we don't know who we are in God, we seek definition through others. But they will always fall short of our expectations.

The third area of needs is security, which is the feeling of being protected and provided for. There are many adults who suffer from insecurity because they never received it as a child while growing up. This is particularly true for people who moved from place to place during their formative years, had parents who separated, or witnessed a father who didn't provide for the family. An unstable home life can really affect a child's sense of personal security. Being shuffled from place to place to live and attend school when parents are separated or divorced can be overwhelming for a child. And when children sense that their parents' agendas are more important than they are, a fear of abandonment can easily invade a child's mind.

> "TO GET PAST THE FEAR OF ABANDONMENT IN RELATIONSHIPS, WE HAVE TO GET OUT OF OUR OWN PERSONAL WORLD OF FEAR AND INSECURITY."

We live in a day and time where single parent homes are increasingly becoming the norm. And there are households where the father (and in some cases the mother) has abandoned the family. If you came from this type of situation, God can restore you. I encourage you to evaluate your life and discover any needs that were not fulfilled. Even in the face of these types of odds, God can meet the need for security like no one else can.

Finally, there is the need for a sense of purpose in life, which is simply knowing you have a reason to live. A lot of people ask the questions: *"What is my purpose?"* and *"What is my reason for living?"* Knowing your purpose means knowing that God has a special plan for your life. There is a reason why each of us was born into the particular family, city, and circumstances we came into. It is all a part of God's divine plan and our personal testimony. You may not know it right now, but God has something awesome prepared for you (Jeremiah 29:11).

I can remember a time in my life when I was battling depression. One day, many years ago, I sat in my garage from morning until evening trying to figure out how to kill myself without going to hell. I am so glad I didn't go through with it because God had a plan and purpose for my life. There is no greater satisfaction in life than to discover your purpose. God has not abandoned us, leaving us to wander through life unaware of the reason we were put on this planet. Whether you think your purpose is big or small, rejoice when you come to the realization that you are not just here by accident. You are a part of a bigger picture, and God needs you.

So when we look at these four needs, we have to understand that God is going to use positive relationships to meet these needs—relationships through which His power and grace will flow, building us up to where He has designed us to be. This is why it is important that we do not run from relationships out of a fear of abandonment.

GOD NEVER LEAVES US

Fear of abandonment in relationships essentially compares to a fear of failure in our dealings with others. We become scared to make any type of investment, or we go through our relationships with the nagging fear that the object of our affection will eventually leave us for something or someone better. The first place to start when working on overcoming this fear is understanding that no matter what our background may have been, or even if none of our core needs were met growing up, God will never leave or forsake us (Hebrews 13:5). Since our relationships with others are largely shaped by how we relate to God, we must begin to look at Him as He really is—a Heavenly Father who wants the best for us and to make us happy. When our feelings toward God are positive, we tend to have a more positive outlook on others, and on life in general. The way we perceive God greatly impacts how we relate to other people.

God is deeply in love with each and every one of us, and a revelation of that love and Who He is flushes fear out of our consciousness. Unfortunately, many of us grew up in negative situations that have caused our concept of God to be either non-existent or severely distorted. We must renew our minds to the nature of God and the fact that He is an actual person Who is aware of every intricate detail of our lives.

God is love (1 John 4:16), and He wants to bring us to a place of ultimate fulfillment. He works through relationships because

He does not want us isolating ourselves from others out of fear. Relationships are bridges to new levels of success and prosperity. We must, however, be able to discern the people in our lives and choose our friends wisely. With the guidance of the Holy Spirit, we can ensure that we invite the loving energy of people who will care for us and meet our needs; however, we must first allow God to be our primary caregiver, where our emotions are concerned. When we know Him as our source, it enables us to be whole so that we do not attract hurtful, broken individuals into our lives.

Proverbs 18:24 says there is a friend who sticks closer than a brother, and that friend is Jesus. Sometimes we become so used to hearing the religious descriptions and concepts of God that we forget the person of Jesus. He is available, and we can depend on Him for comfort, strength, and security at all times. As our closest friend, He opens doors to relationships that reflect His character and nature back to us. When we embrace these relationships, we will begin to see Jesus in the people He has chosen to touch our lives.

To get past the fear of abandonment in relationships, we have to get out of our own personal world of fear and insecurity. We do this by focusing our attention and energy on God and His Word, meditating on it, and acting on it in faith. As we become more Word-conscious and love-conscious, fear will start to leave us. On the other hand, when we wrap ourselves in a protective shield of fear, we are really being selfish. There are things in us God wants to use to bless other people, but when we stay in self-preservation mode, we hinder what the Lord is trying to do through and for us. We must embrace relationships first, and second, we must look at how we can give the advantage to others rather than what we can get out of the deal. Becoming mature in our love walk helps eliminate fear.

So we should want to seek friendship because we are interested in what we can do for someone else. We have to know we are valuable, and be ready to bring something special to the table to help someone else become a better person. This only comes through spending significant time in the Word of God and building ourselves up in it. As we begin to sow into someone else's life, we position ourselves to receive the same thing!

How can we be abandoned if we trust God, walk in love, and sow good seeds into the lives of others? Quite simply, we can't and we won't. If we want people to treat us the way we want to be treated, we have to ask ourselves the question, *"Have I ever sown a seed to get what I desire?"* Remember, relationships are designed to give the advantage to someone else. In every relationship where we refer to someone as our friend, we need to ask ourselves what we are doing to enhance his or her life. This really comes down to an issue of character, because character is doing what is right in order to prosper those with whom we are in relationship.

DOING THINGS THE KINGDOM WAY

Having a consciousness of love and bringing that way of thinking to our relationships is a great way to experience freedom from the fear of abandonment. Think about it, fear causes us to completely focus on self, while love extends toward someone else. We must renew our minds with the love of God if we are ever going to be happy in relationships with others.

Romans 12:1, 2 instructs us to be transformed by the renewing of our minds with the Word so we can prove what is the acceptable and perfect will of God. The world's way of governing relationships is completely fear-based and selfish in that the focus is on self-gratification. When people are broken and have not awakened to the love of God, they carry the wounds from their past into every relationship they encounter. Barriers of hurt and fear keep the blessing of God from manifesting in those situations, and the result is more pain and disappointment. However, when we get in the Word of God and allow it to change us from the inside out, we become open to the possibility that there really are people out there who want to love and care for us. Everyone is not out to get us or leave us just when we thought we could open up.

Abandonment is devastating, and one of the things that comes from it is brokenheartedness. Have you ever met people who have had so many bad relationships that they just don't have any more hope that someone could love them or treat them right? Past rejection, whether from childhood or later on in life, leaves individuals emotionally scarred and reluctant to open up. However, even in the face of devastating past experiences, I want to let you know that there is good news for you. In Luke 4:18, Jesus describes exactly what His mission is, and the results of abandonment are covered: *"The Spirit of the*

Lord is upon me, because he hath anointed me to preach the gospel to the poor, he hath sent me to heal the brokenhearted, to preach deliverance to the captives, and recovering of sight to the blind, to set at liberty them that are bruised."

There are several powerful truths contained in this scripture pertaining to the fear of abandonment and the results that come from not having our core needs met. Jesus says He was sent to heal the brokenhearted. If you have experienced a broken heart because you were abandoned or left when you were most vulnerable, Jesus can heal your wounded heart. You don't have to live with that pain another day.

He also says He came to preach deliverance to the captives. Fear holds us in bondage and keeps us from experiencing the liberty of healthy relationships. Jesus has opened the prison doors and set free those who are in bondage to fear. He has also destroyed the works of the devil, rendering them inoperative against us when we walk in our God-given authority. Are you struggling with fear? Take authority over it, knowing you don't have to remain in that prison cell. You *can* experience love and security in your relationships with others.

He also says He came to give liberty to those who are "bruised." Whenever we experience emotional hardship, particularly when we feel as if we have been left all alone, there is a type of "bruising" that takes place in our spirits. To protect those hurting places, we construct walls of fear that we think are protecting us, when they are actually connecting us to the things we don't want to happen to us. Again, Jesus has made freedom and healing available to us through His love. He paid the price for us to be free from fear of any kind.

In order for us to become strong and confident in God's love, we have to spend time in the Word of God, pray, and seek Him first. When our emotions are ruling our lives, we will make bad decisions. But when we allow God's love to eradicate fear, we will not only receive wonderful relationships in our lives, but we will also find ourselves walking in His divine and perfect will.

Don't be afraid to love. Regardless of what someone has done in the past, God is consistent. He will bless you according to your faith. And when you trust Him completely, the fear of abandonment will not be able to stop what He is bringing into your life. Keep your eyes on Him, and don't be distracted by what the enemy is doing. A bright future, with thriving relationships, await you!

CHAPTER 13
Redeemed from Death

"For God so loved the world, that he gave his only begotten Son,
that whosoever believeth in him should not perish,
but have everlasting life"

(John 3:16).

Death. I'm not sure I can think of a word that communicates as much finality as this word does. It is a topic most people don't like to think about because, to be honest, it can be frightening, especially when they are unsure of what lies beyond their last breath. However, death is real and inescapable; we are all going to come face to face with the reality of death one day, which is why God wants us to be prepared for that moment. His Word provides all the answers we need about life *and* death, and what is next for every human being who passes on. By shining light on the subject of death, we can live our lives with fearless confidence, knowing something wonderful awaits us when we live a life of faith in God and His Word.

All of us have been touched in some way by the death of a friend, loved one, or acquaintance. Whether we had a close relationship with someone who died or not doesn't diminish the reality that he or she is permanently gone from this physical realm, which is a pretty sobering thought. Even more sobering is the idea that he or she did not necessarily make it to heaven.

UNDERSTANDING THE CURSE OF SPIRITUAL DEATH

The account of the fall of man in the book of Genesis is particularly important to understand because it shows how death actually came into being. We first have to understand that mankind was never created to die. Our heavenly Father made man in His image and infused him with the very life of God, intending him to live for eternity in a glorified physical body that was immune to disease or death on any level. This life force, called *zoë*, was what gave man his divine quality; it is what made him "god-like," with the same creative ability as the Father.

God created the first man and woman to remain in perfect fellowship with Him throughout eternity and to flourish on the earth to such a point that it became a physical replication of heaven! Adam and Eve were literally equipped with everything they would need, from a spiritual and physical standpoint, to live forever. Again, their bodies were never created to die. Life in the Garden of Eden was to last throughout eternity.

Unfortunately, Satan was able to corrupt this earthly paradise and disrupt the perfect relationship man had with God by enticing him to sin. Most of us are familiar with the biblical account of what happened when Adam and Eve ate of the fruit of the Tree of the Knowledge of Good and Evil, but I want to back up to God's original instructions to them concerning this tree. In Genesis 2:17 He says, *"But of the tree of the knowledge of good and evil, thou shalt not eat of it: for in the day that thou eatest thereof thou shalt surely die."*

The death God is speaking of here is referring to *spiritual* death. Everything that happens in this natural, physical realm is the result of what goes on in the spiritual realm first. When God said they would surely die, He meant that they would be separated from His very life force, as well as His provision. This was the first phase of death they would experience; the second was the deterioration of their bodies—a curse that all human beings would eventually experience.

So when Adam and Eve disobeyed God by eating the forbidden fruit, they immediately were cut off from the zoë life of God. Spiritual death entered their spirits, where love and life once flowed from the Father to them. The curse entered the earth and these two people, who once enjoyed a life of complete and perfect union with God, now became ruled and governed by fear, death, sin, and disease. Their undefiled relationship with the Father was corrupted. Genesis 3:23, 24 says, *"Therefore the Lord God sent him forth from the garden of Eden, to till the ground from whence he was taken. So he drove out the man..."* They were not only banished from the Garden of Eden, but the spiritual death that infected them would now infect all of humanity.

What a horrible price to pay for disobedience!

So here we have the first man and woman now carrying the curse of spiritual (and physical) death. By handing their authority over to Satan, they entered into the death cycle. All of mankind would be spiritually disconnected from God by the mere fact that we are descendants of Adam (Psalm 51:5). Thankfully, not even Adam and Eve's grave mistake could separate them from the love of God. He made a provision for us all to escape the clutches of spiritual death and enter back into eternal life with Him through Jesus Christ.

Before getting into a discussion of hell, I want to explain what happened when Jesus died on the cross for us. John 3:16, 17 says, "*For God so loved the world, that he gave his only begotten Son, that whosoever believeth in him should not perish, but have everlasting life. For God sent not his Son into the world to condemn the world; but that the world through him might be saved.*"

Jesus came to the earth, preached the message of salvation, and subjected Himself to the crucifixion, the curse of death, and the pains of hell before He rose from the grave so that you and I might be brought back into perfect fellowship with the Father. He was *made* sin so that we could *become* the righteousness of God. When Jesus died on the cross, He took our place so we wouldn't have to be punished for our spiritual condition. When we accept Jesus into our hearts by faith, believing that He is the Son of God who died for our sins and was raised from the dead, we come into right relationship with the Father once again.

To be "saved" means to be rescued from the curse of sin and its effects on this earth and after death. As Christians, we now have the life of God flowing through us and energizing our spirits; we are no longer spiritually dead men and women. We have access to the supernatural power of God right now, and we have the power to live a life that lines up with His Word, through the Holy Spirit who now dwells in us. Accepting Jesus allows us to be spiritually "born again," from death to life, and grants us access to heaven. This means, when we die, our bodies become lifeless but our spirits immediately go on to be with the Father forever. Our eternal destination is now secure.

THE DESTINATION OF
THE SPIRITUALLY DEAD

No one wants to accept the fact that he or his loved ones may go to hell after they die. If we don't understand the truth about sin and what it means to be born again, we will get defensive at the very mention of hell. The idea that we may not be as "good" as we think we are is a hard pill to swallow, but unless we see ourselves the way God does, we will be deceived into accepting a lot of ideas about life after death that don't line up with the Word.

The issue of who is going to hell has nothing to do with how good or bad a person is, per se, and more to do with the spiritual nature of a person before he or she dies. You see, no matter how many good works we do in this life, or how good we think we are, we simply do not qualify for heaven without having accepted Jesus Christ and becoming spiritually reborn. His blood sacrifice is what makes an eternity in heaven possible for every man and woman on the face of the planet. All it takes is receiving the free gift of salvation as an act of our will.

It is the recreated, regenerated spirit that is quickened and made alive by faith in Jesus that gains access to heaven after the body dies. Without Jesus, we simply cannot make it in, not so much because of what we have done, but because of our spiritually dead nature that is ruled by the law of sin and death. In the presence of a holy God, sin is annihilated, which is why becoming born again is so critical to our eternal futures. No one gains access to the Father except through Jesus Christ (John 14:6).

With that being said, what happens to those who choose not to accept Jesus as their Lord and personal Savior while they are still alive? Let's look to the Word for the answer. First, we must understand that every one of us is a tri-part being, meaning we are a spirit, we possess a soul, and we live in a physical body. The spirit of a man is what animates his or her body. A great way to look at physical death is through the illustration of a person wearing a suit. As long as someone is wearing the suit, it has form and can move. But the moment he takes the suit off, it simply lies where it is, unable to move on its own.

This is how it is when we die. The real you is a spirit being, and your body is your "earth suit," which enables you to have contact with this physical realm. Your soul includes your mind, will, and emotions, and is where you think, feel, and make decisions. So when we die, the spirit and soul (which are attached) separate from the body and move on to the next phase of existence called eternity. The person you see lying in a casket at a funeral is not really that person! In actuality, the death of the physical body is not the end of a person's existence; he or she still exists, only in a spiritual form.

For the person who is born again, the Bible says "to be absent from the body is to be present with the Lord." What a comforting thought! Those who die in the Lord go to heaven, a place of unimaginable beauty, peace, joy, and everlasting

> "NOTHING ANY ONE OF US HAS EVER DONE CAN SEPARATE US FROM THE LOVE OF GOD OR THE TRANSFORMING POWER OF JESUS' BLOOD."

happiness. However, people who die without making Jesus the Lord of their lives, sadly, go to a horrible place called hell.

An example of what happens when we die in a spiritually dead state can be found in Luke 16:19-25. In this passage of scripture, there is a man who died and went to hell. It says:

> *"There was a certain rich man, which was clothed in purple and fine linen, and fared sumptuously every day: And there was a certain beggar named Lazarus, which was laid at his gate, full of sores, And desiring to be fed with the crumbs which fell from the rich man's table: moreover the dogs came*

and licked his sores. And it came to pass , that the beggar died, and was carried by the angels into Abraham's bosom: the rich man also died, and was buried; And in hell he lift up his eyes, being in torments, and seeth Abraham afar off, and Lazarus in his bosom. And he cried and said, Father Abraham, have mercy on me, and send Lazarus, that he may dip the tip of his finger in water, and cool my tongue; for I am tormented in this flame. But Abraham said, Son, remember that thou in thy lifetime receivedst thy good things, and likewise Lazarus evil things: but now he is comforted, and thou art tormented."

When a person dies, he goes to his eternal home—heaven or hell. The rich man in this passage was in hell, and he could still feel things. When we die, we will have spiritual bodies, and our souls will still be intact, meaning our five senses will still be functioning. In fact, everything we see, hear, touch, taste, and feel will be heightened because the spiritual realm is more real than the natural, physical realm. The only thing we won't have is the ability to choose our destination. Once we die, we are locked into eternity, and our destinies are irreversible.

Hell is a real place, and it was never intended for mankind. God created hell for the devil and his angels, but unfortunately, those who reject Jesus Christ will end up in that horrible place by default, being tormented throughout eternity. The good news is that *none* of us has to go there! We have complete control over where we go when we die, which eradicates a lot of the fear associated with death. Salvation does, however, require faith on our part to believe in the power of Jesus' blood and acceptance of Him as our Lord and Savior. By entering into the family of God through the "door" of Jesus Christ, we can live free from the fear of being eternally separated from God after we die.

REDEEMED FROM SPIRITUAL DEATH

I often marvel at the depth, height, and extent of God's love, and I pray that I gain even more insight into this love every day. One of the things that really strikes me as phenomenal is how God loved us so much that He came up with a plan to rectify the issue of spiritual death in mankind, even before any of us were born! Through His Son, Jesus, He has redeemed each and every one of us from an eternity of torment, death, and destruction. He has also given us the gift of free will so that we can choose where we go after we die.

Make no mistake about it, death is not the end of our existence; it is actually the beginning because it marks the genesis of our entrance into eternity, where time ceases to exist. In these last days, there will be all kinds of teachings and beliefs about what happens after we die, and we must guard against the wrong information. Some believe in reincarnation while others believe that death simply equates to an eternal sleep in which we are basically unconscious. Be not deceived. Any information that did not originate from God's Word is designed to lead you away from the truth. None of these beliefs about death are accurate.

The death of our bodies does not mean our spirits and souls cease to exist. Heaven and hell are real locations, places that exist beyond the physical realm. If we choose Jesus, believing in what His blood has accomplished for us, we will go to heaven. If we reject Him during our lifetime, we will go to hell—it's just that simple. When the day comes that we must give an account of our lives to God, we will not be able to escape the fact that we had a choice in the matter. God doesn't choose our futures for us; we do. Knowing this allows us to take our place in God's Kingdom without fear of any kind.

Romans 8:14-16 gives insight to the reality of living a fear-free life as a Believer because of our new nature. It says, *"For as many as are led by the Spirit of God, they are the sons of God. For ye have not received the spirit of bondage again to fear; but ye have received the Spirit of adoption, whereby we cry, Abba, Father. The Spirit itself beareth witness with our spirit, that we are the children of God."* What a powerful statement! Hebrews 2:14, 15 also says, *"Forasmuch then as the children are partakers of flesh and blood, he also himself likewise took part of the same; that through death he might destroy him that had the power of death, that is, the devil; And deliver them who through fear of death were all their lifetime subject to bondage."*

The fear of death brings lifelong bondage, but when you are a child of God, you are no longer subject to the spirit of bondage that comes with fear. To be afraid of death is really to be ignorant of your status as a child of God, according to these scriptures. Take confidence in the truth of God's Word! When you are born again, you become disconnected from the fear of death and reconnected with the life and love of God. You have nothing to fear when He lives in your heart.

It is my desire that every person I encounter be impacted with the truth about God's love. Nothing any one of us has done can separate us from the love of God or the transforming power of Jesus' blood. Through His blood, we can be recreated in our spirits so that we have access to the Father's presence. He has made a way out of fear and a way out of eternal damnation. Life doesn't end with our last breath, but our last breath can be the beginning of a beautiful and bright future with God that lasts throughout eternity. Choose Jesus today and secure your ultimate destination. There is no fear in God, who is love. He has redeemed you from spiritual death!

CHAPTER 14
Conquering the Fear of Failure

"Blessed be the God and Father of our Lord Jesus Christ, who hath blessed us with all spiritual blessings in heavenly places in Christ"

(Ephesians 1:3).

There is a popular slogan used by a well-known athletic company that says, "Just do it." It is a phrase that speaks of fearlessness and confidence, one that communicates a sense of taking immediate action. For many people, the idea of "just doing it" is frightening, to say the least. Past failures often keep them from stepping out on their dreams or trying something new. The fear of failure is an absolute hindrance to progress because it paralyzes us from moving forward. Fortunately, the freedom from fear that is available through a relationship with God covers the fear of failure. We *can* just do it when we have understanding of the empowerment that comes through the blessing of God.

I remember when the Lord first spoke to me about starting World Changers Church International. He gave me a vision of the World Dome, and I remember wondering how it would all come together. I'm sure you can imagine the range of emotions I went through when I received God's vision—fear and uncertainty definitely tried to rise up in my mind. However, I learned that when it comes to stepping out on something God is telling us to do, it is going to take faith. That is a major key to being able to see our dreams come to fruition.

Where does the fear of failure come from? It comes from Satan. Whenever we experience a negative emotion that tries to stop us from moving forward, we have to recognize that it does not come from God. It is the result of words the enemy injects in our minds, which we receive and fail to deal with. Once those words, spoken through others or through Satan himself, begin to take root in our thinking, our feelings will be affected as well. It won't be long before we start acting in ways that sabotage our own progress.

The only person who wants us to fail in life is the devil, which is why he pulls out all the stops to make sure our mindsets are so saturated with fear and doubt that we remain where we are. All of us have a purpose, direction, and calling from God, which means there is something specific He has for us to do. The visions, aspirations, talents, and natural strengths we have often coincide with the purpose He has for us. Not only that, but the things God has for us to do are *always* going to be bigger than our ability to do them on our own. Accepting that the vision will always supersede our own ability will keep us in a position of having to trust and rely on God to help us.

When it came to starting a church, I had no idea where to begin. I couldn't rely on my own knowledge because I had never done anything like this before. While I had a lot to learn on my journey toward the will of God for my life, I had to begin somewhere; I had to step out on what God told me to do, regardless of how fear tried to creep into my mind. World Changers began in the cafeteria of a local elementary school with only a few people in attendance. In fact, there were times when I preached to empty chairs! Taking a leap of faith was the first step for me, but it was worth it. God has done everything He said He would do and more.

EMPOWERED TO HAVE SUCCESS

God has not left us alone without any "equipment" to help us accomplish our goals. On the contrary, He has bestowed upon every person who is in the Kingdom of God something called *the blessing*. Many times people equate the word *blessing* with material wealth and tangible objects of prosperity, such as money, houses, and cars; however, the blessing is much more than these things.

To be blessed means to be empowered to prosper and have success. The blessing is actually a supernatural empowerment or enabling that comes from God. When we are blessed, we are successful in life, and it is evident to those around us. Renewing our minds to cultivate a blessing consciousness is vital to obtaining victory over the fear of failure.

How did the blessing come into being and how do we gain access to it? First of all, Adam and Eve were both equipped with the blessing when God created them. Genesis 1:27, 28 says that God created man in His image and *blessed* them, charging them to be fruitful, multiply, replenish the earth, and have dominion over it. That sure doesn't sound like failure to me! No, God gave mankind the spiritual tool he needed to have supernatural success. That tool was the blessing!

Now, we know that Adam and Eve disobeyed God in the Garden of Eden, and the results of their sin included spiritual separation from God, and the curse. The blessing was disrupted because of their disobedience, but it was reinstated through God's covenant relationship with Abraham, who provided the lineage through which Jesus would be born. Ephesians 1:3 says, "*Blessed be the God and Father of our Lord Jesus Christ, who hath blessed us with all spiritual blessings in heavenly places in Christ.*" All spiritual blessings mean *everything* we could possibly need to be successful in life from a spiritual and natural perspective.

When I think of empowerment, I think of absolute mastery over every circumstance and situation in life. It brings to mind the idea of confidence and a positive outlook because of what we have already been equipped with. When you *know* the blessing is resting on your life, you have no reason to fear failure. God will back up the blessing with tangible results.

THE SPIRIT OF MIGHT

As Believers we have access to the multi-faceted power of

God every moment of the day. That is exciting news! How can fear stand in the presence of the love of God? It can't. Isaiah 11:2 describes seven aspects of God's power that are at our disposal: *"And the spirit of the Lord shall rest upon him, the spirit of wisdom and understanding, the spirit of counsel and might, the spirit of knowledge and of the fear of the Lord."* The facet I want to focus on here is the spirit of might. It is what gives us the edge and advantage when it comes to stepping out on what we are afraid to do.

What is might? It is the ability to do *anything*. Might is released through the knowledge of the Word of God. When we know what God has already declared about us, it bolsters our confidence and empowers us to step out because we can do nothing *except* succeed. The enemy cannot stand against the spirit of might when it comes on a Christian who is walking by faith. The question is, are you willing to spend enough time in the Word until you gain a deep, abiding understanding of who you are and how you have been blessed? It is only through revelation knowledge that you will be unshakeable in your faith.

There are many instances in the Bible when the spirit of might was in operation. One powerful example is when Jesus was able to endure extreme torture in His physical body and still continue on in His mission to complete what God had called Him to do. Jesus suffered immense physical trauma, which most people would not have been able to bear. In fact, the first phase of His execution began when He was scourged. From a physical standpoint, most people who were scourged did not even come out of it alive. Jesus' body was literally ripped apart from the whippings and beatings he suffered at the hands of the Roman soldiers, *before* He was forced to carry His cross and be subjected to one of the most excruciatingly painful executions known to man. When I think about what Jesus went through, it amazes me that He lasted as long as He did. How was He able to accomplish it? It was through the spirit of might. It was the blessing empowerment that enabled Him to do what is impossible in the natural.

Thinking about Jesus and how the spirit of might gave Him the strength to fulfill His assignment as the Savior of mankind really puts things in perspective when I think of the things God has called me to do that may seem impossible. But none of us will ever have to carry out an assignment to the magnitude of what Jesus did. I sometimes think about the things that may have gone through His mind

> "KNOW THAT, WITH THE SPIRIT OF MIGHT AND THE BLESSING OF GOD ON YOUR SIDE, NOTHING CAN STOP YOU."

from a human perspective. The thought of what was before Him had to be overwhelming. His human side undoubtedly feared He would not be able to go through with it. Remember, Jesus was just as much man as He was God, which means He was not immune to the negative emotions and suggestions of the devil that we encounter.

The Bible gives the account of Jesus in the Garden of Gethsemane, which is also known as "the passion" or "agony" of

Jesus. This was where the enemy waged spiritual warfare with Him to get Him to quit on what He was called to do. I am sure the enemy plagued His mind with the fear of failure; however, Jesus didn't give in to the mental suggestions of Satan. Instead, He reacted just as He did when Satan tempted Him in the wilderness. Jesus defeated Satan with the Word of God and through His faith.

Mark 14:32-36 says:

> And they came to a place which was named Gethsemane: and he saith to his disciples, Sit ye here, while I shall pray. And he taketh with him Peter and James and John, and began to be sore amazed, and to be very heavy; And saith unto them, My soul is exceeding sorrowful unto death: tarry ye here, and watch. And he went forward a little, and fell on the ground, and prayed that, if it were possible, the hour might pass from him. And he said, Abba, Father, all things are possible unto thee; take away this cup from me: nevertheless not what I will, but what thou wilt.

The *Amplified* version of this scripture says Jesus was "struck with terror and amazement and deeply troubled and depressed. He even said His soul was exceedingly sad and overwhelmed with grief to the point where it almost killed Him! I don't know about you, but that sounds like the fear of failure to me, among a host of other negative emotions trying to get Jesus to quit.

That's exactly what Satan does to us isn't it? He tries to get us to become so overwhelmed with what is before us that we doubt we can even begin to carry it out. But the blessing on our lives and the spirit of might is what enables us to move forward. Jesus tapped into that power that night in the Garden. It is what gave Him the strength to carry out His assignment, and we have been empowered with the same ability. We can do *anything* through this blessing that rests on our lives.

The Word of God consistently backs up the truth about the supernatural ability we possess. The Apostle Paul's confidence in what He had been equipped with was evident in his declaration, "*I can do all things through Christ which strengtheneth me.*" His attitude here definitely was one of victory, not defeat. With everything he had to face when it came to preaching the Gospel, many times in hostile lands, it was imperative for him to hold on to the revelation of empowerment. The fear of failure simply could not be entertained if he was to successfully accomplish what he had been called to do.

JUST DO IT!

I am so grateful for the Word of God because it holds the answers to overcoming every inner battle we will experience. Moving beyond the fear of failure involves three basic steps which, if followed, will produce results.

I. **Take authority.**

Every Christian has been given supernatural power over Satan and his wicked forces. Knowing our authority is critical. When fearful thoughts come, refuse to accept them and take authority over them immediately. Enforce your victory over fear by speaking the Word of God. Luke 10:19 says, *"Behold, I give unto you power to tread on serpents and scorpions, and over all the power of the enemy: and nothing shall by any means hurt you."* You hold the power to expel the devil from your mind, so let him know who the boss is the moment he attacks.

2. **Recognize that you have been empowered to succeed in life.** Developing a "blessing" consciousness is one of the most important things we can do to overcome the fear of failure. This has to be a total life attitude that we carry with us at all times and in every situation. Becoming confident in the empowerment with which God has equipped us comes through constant meditation of the Word, until it begins to affect us on a subconscious level. When we renew our minds to the fact that there is an anointing available for us to do *all* things, it will shape the way we see and approach seemingly insurmountable challenges. Instead of being afraid to step out, we will be eager to move forward.

3. **Step out.** Once you have taken care of the spiritual aspects of fear, the next thing to do is step out! It is one thing to say you are no longer scared of failing, but the acid test is whether you put action to that belief. Faith without works is dead, which means you have *to* do something to back up what you believe. It is in the practical expression of your faith in

God's Word that confidence is demonstrated. Step out in faith by resting in the finished works of Jesus. Your work is to labor to enter into His rest (Hebrews 4:10, 11).

THE FAITH TO SUCCEED

Everything in the Kingdom of God operates by faith, which means that we are going to always have to use faith to appropriate what grace has already made available to us. The vision God gives us will always be bigger than we are because He wants us to always have to depend on Him.

The Israelites in Numbers Chapter 13 certainly feared failure when it came to possessing the land God promised them. It was rightfully theirs, but intimidation was lurking in their minds. When the twelve spies went to Canaan to survey the land, they returned to Moses and Caleb with a bad report that was based on what they saw: "*And they brought up an evil report of the land which they had searched unto the children of Israel, saying, The land, through which we have gone to search it, is a land that eateth up the inhabitants thereof; and all the people that we saw in it are men of a great stature...and we were in our own sight as grasshoppers, and so we were in their sight.*" (vv.32, 33).

In spite of the negative report they brought back, I love what Caleb said in verse 30, "*...Let us go up at once, and possess it; for we are well able to overcome it.*" That sounds like an attitude that is governed by the spirit of might to me! Caleb not only refused to accept the bad report, but he wanted his people to immediately move into action! In essence he was saying to the Israelites, "Let's just do it!"

It takes faith to succeed in life—faith in God's love for us that no matter what we may be up against, no matter how big the challenges look, we possess something bigger than the challenge. Our faith, backed by the blessing of God, is what unlocks the door to ultimate success and victory in life. We must adopt a Caleb mindset and attitude in every situation we face. This is the winner's attitude, who doesn't look at the hurdle, but sees the end from the beginning.

I don't know what your vision or dream is, but if God gave it to you, it requires faith to come to pass. Begin filling up on the Word so your degree of confidence can rise high enough to move you into action. Know that with the spirit of might and the blessing of God on your side, nothing can stop you. The fear of failure has no place in the life of a Believer who knows what God has made available to him. Whatever it is God has called you to do— just do it! Your success is inevitable.

CHAPTER 15
Pornography: Fear of Real Intimacy in Action

"The heart is deceitful above all things,
and desperately wicked: who can know it?"

(Jeremiah 17:9).

If you drive down most busy city streets in metropolitan areas across the country, there is one thing you are sure to see—the flashing lights of adult entertainment establishments. There is no shortage of sexually explicit material available to the general public at any given time. Whether it is the neighborhood strip club, the pornography shop that sells hardcore movies and magazines, or XXX rated websites on the Internet, pornography has become commonplace in society today. In fact, it is a multi-billion dollar industry that continues to grow in response to the lustful demands of the public. Pornographers and many involved in the sex industry push the lie that says this type of entertainment is harmless fun, but in reality it is far from harmless. Truthfully, pornography is merely an attempt to create the illusion of intimacy, while falling terribly short of that goal. It is actually born out of a *fear* of real intimacy with others, and ultimately leads to emotional isolation and despair.

How does a person become hooked on pornography, and what role does fear play in that process? In order to understand this better, we must first look at the heart of man and how a person's carnal desires, which are based in selfishness, are used by the enemy to draw them into addictive behavior. Jeremiah 17:9 says something very interesting, *"The heart is deceitful above all things, and desperately wicked: who can know it?"* When he talks about the "heart" here, he is referring to the spirit of a man that is ruled by carnality, along with the unrenewed mind, also known as the "flesh." All of us possessed this unrenewed spirit before becoming born again, and as a result, we were subject to the lusts and appetites that were a natural part of it. When we get saved, our spirits are recreated and are reconnected to the life of God, making us free from sin; however, even after we accept Jesus, though our spirits are recreated, our minds are not. All the fearful, selfish desires that were inherent to our carnal nature must be continually put to death as an act of our will. We do this by making a conscious decision to choose God's way instead of our old ways. By meditating and acting on the Scriptures consistently, we are able to "walk in the Spirit" and keep ourselves from fulfilling the lusts of our flesh.

With that being said, loneliness, fear, and emptiness are all part of the curse of negative emotions that came on mankind during the Fall. As a result, there is a natural tendency to go in the direction of these emotions when we go through hard times. The enemy constantly magnifies these feelings through failed relationships, unmet needs, and negative encounters with others who have hurt us. When we don't use the Word to counter such things, we will be open and susceptible to the suggestions and temptations of the devil, pornography being one of them. Anything that seems to provide a temporary way of escape from emotional pain is designed to trap us. We must be sure that we have a relationship with Jesus Christ and that we also initiate and continue the process of renewing our minds.

Staying focused on the Word of God is going to be the key to dealing with the worldly enticements that bombard our senses every day. We will always be presented with opportunities to become self-centered rather than God-centered. If we don't turn to the Word to deal with distress, we will find other ways to do it. Let's examine exactly what pornography is, its objective, and how people become vulnerable to it.

CREATING FALSE INTIMACY THROUGH SELF-CENTEREDNESS

Pornography is defined in *Webster's Dictionary* as pictures, writing, or films designed to arouse sexual excitement. Pornography is everywhere, and with the Internet readily available, one click of a mouse can give adults, teens, and children access to some of the most hardcore pornographic images. Pornography is not limited to the aforementioned items, however. Places like strip clubs feed the pornographic mindset as well. The root word for pornography is the Greek word *porneia* which means "prostitution; idolatry; fornication; adultery; homosexuality; lesbianism; etc." (www.studylight.org, *The New Testament Greek Lexicon*) Sexual fantasies, created by pornography, are a form of idolatry because they involve a devotion to man's ability to fabricate a solution to fulfilling his needs without God. It is essentially the worship of "self" in every way, and is a deviation from the godly worship the Lord requires of us.

Anytime we violate the commandment of love, fear is automatically present. When we seek to take care of our needs outside of God, we are far from walking in love, and since love is what casts out fear, we can't be selfish and expect to be free from fear's torment. Fear will always infiltrate our lives when we are operating in selfishness.

Selfishness is not often considered in the area of emotional needs, but it is real. All of us have a need for relationships because we were not created to be islands that exist apart from others. We want to be loved, accepted, and made to feel special. When we do not receive this affirmation growing up, we may feel empty inside, and as a result, we can easily lose focus of God if there is nothing to counter those negative emotions.

Often, it is our painful past experiences that cause us to become fearful of opening up to people on a deeply emotional level, and that thrusts us into a life of emotional self-preservation. Who hasn't been through the heartache of a broken relationship or hurt caused by a parent in some way? Regardless of what happened, none of these things give us the license to be selfish; God still wants us to run to Him for comfort and support. Unfortunately, for many people, pornography has become a way of escape from the relational loneliness they feel as a result of their seeming inability to have meaningful relationships, or even because of what they perceive as some lack of fulfillment in a current relationship. Too often we become preoccupied with looking at what someone else isn't doing for *us* rather than looking for ways to bless *them,* and we lose sight of the purpose of relationships—to give the advantage to others. When we retreat to a place of self-preservation, selfish-gratification is often the result.

Make no mistake about it; pornography is all about fear and selfishness. It is a way to receive a sense of intimacy without having to risk being hurt by another person.

Users are seeking personal satisfaction in the area of their emotional needs, and instead of allowing God to take care of these needs His way, they choose pictures, images, and fantasies. The smiling woman in a pornographic magazine is non-threatening and incapable of inflicting emotional pain. She also requires no investment of emotion, time, or effort on the part of the viewer. As an object of sexual desire, her only

> "TRUTHFULLY, PORNOGRAPHY IS MERELY AN ATTEMPT TO CREATE THE ILLUSION OF INTIMACY, WHILE FALLING TERRIBLY SHORT OF THAT GOAL."

purpose in the mind of the viewer is to provide sexual pleasure.

To a person who has created a fictional world of self-gratification, the objectified woman seems like the ideal answer to the fear of being hurt. Sexual fantasies can create a seemingly perfect world of nourishment, love, and tenderness, as well as images of what the viewer deems necessary for acceptance, self-worth, and a sense of control. People who engage in addictive sexual behavior tend to justify their actions by convincing themselves that their needs *must* be met at any cost. They don't want to feel rejection, so they set up their world to cater to self-gratification. When we turn to things like pornography, we are essentially saying, "God, I don't believe you can take care of this pain. I'm afraid Your way really isn't going to get the job done in my life." As a result of thinking this way, we end up going the way of our flesh. Unfortunately, every encounter with pornography only leaves the individual involved feeling more empty and ashamed.

A person who uses such materials is completely self-centered because at the moment he decides to become involved with a sexual act involving pornography, his drive to satisfy his lust demonstrates a lack of concern for anyone but himself. People who indulge in adult entertainment are not really concerned about how other people are affected by their behavior because meeting their selfish needs is what matters most to them. And the fact that the women who are featured in these movies and magazines are being exploited is not considered either.

As I mentioned earlier, anytime we seek something or someone outside of God to fulfill our needs, we will *always* come up tremendously short. This is because God created each of us with a space inside that only *He* can fill. All of us will experience disappointment; however, pornography is merely a quick fix. The fear of real relationships and the disappointment that is possible with *real* intimacy with another human being are what keep people in a vicious cycle of self-destructive behavior.

While turning the pages of a pornographic magazine or viewing a hardcore movie, a person may feel as if he is being satisfied. The buildup of sexual tension leading to an orgasm from watching pornography only provides a temporary release. Often, the illusion of what is being viewed becomes more real than life itself! However, this is merely an attempt to manage the painful reality of loneliness and emptiness.

False intimacy is Satan's counterfeit of the relationship God wants to have with each of us. The whole objective of pornography is to get us to worship Satan on the altar of selfishness. The enemy tries to get us to feel so isolated and hopeless that the only things that seem attractive are what he has to offer. When we try to fulfill our God-given need for intimacy, while ignoring the root issues that come from not having a thriving relationship with Jesus Christ, we end up with the very opposite of what we are striving to achieve. Often, it is easier to hide behind pretense than repent of our sins and go through the process of healing and deliverance. Trying to escape negative emotions through things like pornography is futile.

I have counseled men who struggle with pornography (both married and single) and the problem is widespread, especially in the body of Christ. So many Believers have given their minds and bodies over to the spirit of lust and are not sure how to get out of it. But there is good news today! Jesus has made a way out of every sexual temptation and sin known to man. In fact, the Word says He was tempted in *all* points, just as we are. Knowing this is very reassuring when it comes to tackling the ugly parts of ourselves we don't want to face. When it comes to becoming free from pornography there are several steps to take to ensure deliverance.

1. **Repent.**

The Bible says the spirit is willing, but the flesh is weak. As I mentioned before, the "flesh" is that part of us that is unrenewed and rebellious to the things of God. It is our carnal nature that constantly fights against the recreated spirit. If given a chance, the flesh will completely take over our lives; it has a mind of its own. For this reason, it is imperative that we recognize when we have allowed our flesh to gain the upper hand, and then repent.

Keep in mind that repentance is not merely saying, "I'm sorry," but it is making a 180-degree turn away from the sin. It means we turn our backs altogether on that particular thing and run in the direction of the Word. It also means doing what is necessary to enforce our decision. Many times we genuinely feel bad about our actions or thoughts, but we haven't truly come to a place of godly sorrow, or brokenness before God. In order for true change to take place, we must become disgusted with the things in our lives that displease the Lord. We must come to Him with a sense of desperation, realizing that if He doesn't meet our needs, we cannot receive ultimate fulfillment.

Repentance is a critical step in the process of experiencing change on a deep, internal level.

People tend to deal with the outward manifestations of sin without taking an honest look at what is in their hearts. Lust and lasciviousness reside in the heart and in order for these things to grow they must be fed regularly. The choice to feed ungodly desires is in our hands, which means *we* play a large part in the situations in which we find ourselves. God is not going to *make* us throw the magazines and hardcore DVDs away. He is not going to force us to not visit pornographic websites. These actions are completely up to us. We must be honest with ourselves and *decide* to "starve" our flesh from the things it wants and has grown accustomed to.

2. **Recognize that choosing selfishness means choosing fear.**

Selfishness cannot be separated from fear. A person who uses pornography may not be consciously aware that he is fearful of anything, but he is actually harboring fear on many levels. Sexual fantasies are an attempt to fill ourselves with passion and numb the reality of being disappointed. Self-gratification is all about preserving "self," and that, in and of itself, speaks of the fear of lack. Whether it is the fear of lacking emotional fulfillment, the fear of not being accepted, the fear of being hurt, or the fear of engaging in relationships where risk is involved, there is no escaping the reality that fear is active in the life of a person who seeks out pornographic images to satisfy his needs. Because fear is such a dangerous spiritual force, realizing it is present is critical to getting rid of it.

3. Decide to choose the love of God.

The great commandment Jesus gave us is to love God with all our heart, soul, mind, and strength, and to love our neighbor as ourselves. As human beings, we are in a constant battle between choosing love over selfishness. This is the whole goal of Christian development. Every day we are faced with opportunities to make this decision, and many times we fail. However, the love of God is greater than our failures; nothing can separate us from it. Jesus is waiting with open arms to help us during our times of weakness if we will only make a decision to choose the love route. We cannot love God and people while viewing pornographic material or objectifying others in our minds.

Acknowledging our own selfishness is the first step. Then, we must make a decision to develop the fruit of the Spirit listed in Galatians 5:22, 23. Verse 24 says those who belong to Christ have *crucified* the flesh with its affections and lust. Sexual fantasies that are based on lustful images only feed the carnal appetites God wants us to kill. Turning away from these things and replacing them with the Word of God strengthens our spirits and gives us the power to overcome temptation. The more we cultivate the fruit of the Spirit, which is love, the more we demonstrate the character of God, and fear cannot stand in His presence.

4. Seek help.

People who are serious about overcoming their fears and getting pornography out of their lives for good, should seek help. God has provided three areas through which we can receive healing and deliverance: His Word, the Holy Spirit, and the people of God.

The Word is the only thing that has the power to penetrate the darkest heart with the light of truth. Hebrews 4:12 says it is quick, powerful, and sharper than *any* two-edged sword. Through the Word, God is able to perform spiritual surgery on our hearts, exposing and cutting away everything that is destroying our lives. It is the spiritual ammunition we need to defeat lust and all types of sexual addictions. By planting the Word in our hearts, through meditating, speaking, and acting on it, a person is able to clearly see the error in their behavior and effectively deal with it.

The Holy Spirit is the second resource we need to assist in deliverance from pornography use. Keep in mind that pornographic materials are poison to a person's spirit, and they pollute the soul with lust and sexual uncleanness. Thankfully, Jesus said the Holy Spirit has been sent to help us in every area of our lives; we are not alone. He searches our hearts and helps us identify the sin that is hindering our spiritual growth.

Psalm 139:23, 24 says, "*Search me, O God, and know my heart: try me, and know my thoughts: And see if there be any wicked way in me, and lead me in the way everlasting.*" Every day we must cry out to God like the psalmist in this passage of Scripture. When we ask the Holy Spirit to take a penetrating look at our hearts, He will show us exactly what is going on inside, enabling us to take the necessary action to become free.

Finally, we must take advantage of the strength and support that is available to us in the body of Christ. Other Believers who are strong in faith and know the Word of God can help us when we struggle and fall. We must be willing to be transparent enough to share what we are going through, because without others we would not be able to make it through. There are many Believers who have been through similar battles and have overcome, and they must also be willing to step in and help a brother or sister who is struggling in the same area.

Hebrews 3:12, 13 talks about how we should encourage one another daily. The Apostle Paul is clearly emphasizing here the importance of Believers fellowshipping with one another. It is within the context of this fellowship that trust is established and healing can begin to take place. Not only that, but building relationships with other Christians creates accountability and responsibility. Allowing others to help bear the burdens of our struggles is an invaluable tool that must be utilized in the process of deliverance.

5. **Allow prayer to create the intimacy you long for.**

One of the major ways we develop intimacy with God is through our prayer life, which is exactly what Satan wants to disrupt and replace with counterfeit intimacy attempts through pornography. Instead of allowing our "secret places" to be the privacy of our living rooms, offices, and darkened clubs where no one can see us indulge in pornographic fantasies, we must turn our secret places into our intimate time with the Lord.

Fellowshipping with God in prayer is the perfect way to be filled and re-filled with His love, wisdom, and grace. It is in that place and time of prayer that we receive the power to conquer the enemy. He strengthens and establishes us in faith, love, and joy. Only through Him can we experience lasting satisfaction, which is why taking time every day to commune with Him in prayer is so vital to our lives.

BE PATIENT

We must remember that change is a process, not a one-time event. Fear will always try to attack our minds, but how we deal with it makes the difference. False intimacy deceives us into believing we can somehow achieve the warmth that comes from a loving relationship with God, through an image on a computer screen, a picture in a magazine, or a trip to a strip club; however, God wants us to turn our backs on anything that is a counterfeit of His love. When we confront the sin and fear in our lives, we will find ourselves experiencing a deeper, more intimate relationship with the Father.

Psalm 73:25 says, *"Whom have I in heaven but you?"* This is what our heart's cry should be every moment of the day. By denying ourselves the selfish desires of our flesh, such as pornography, we position ourselves to love God and others, and we drive fear out of our lives. Only then will the abundant, fulfilling life God has planned for us be attained.

CHAPTER 16
Phobias: When Fear Takes Over Our Emotions

"For God hath not given us the spirit of fear;
but of power, and of love, and of a sound mind"
(2 Timothy 1:7).

Have you ever known someone who had an unusual repulsion or anxiety attack over a particular thing? Perhaps you deal with the same thing yourself and can't seem to figure out how to overcome it. Phobias plague people of all backgrounds and walks of life, often driving them to take actions most may consider extreme, in an attempt to control their environments and avoid whatever they are afraid of. Clearly it is not God's will for people to be afraid of *anything,* especially the things *He* has created. Phobias are simply another manifestation of fear, and if left unchecked, they will not only significantly diminish the quality of our lives, but they will also lead to greater and more serious problems later on. Fear, in any form, is never okay.

Believe it or not, there are at least 1,000 known phobias that range from the fear of needles to the fear of chickens! While most people contend with different degrees of various phobias, for thousands of people, phobias can be devastating and can severely affect their normal day-to-day lives. While some phobias are more common than others, such as the fear of flying, the fear of needles, or the fear of bugs, there are others which are less common, such as the fear of being touched and the fear of germs.

A phobia is defined as a "persistent, illogical fear." This irrational fear is driven by our emotions and causes panic. Because fear is a spiritual force, will-power and psychological effort do little to effectively deal with it.

Phobias are a prime example of the bondage that is attached to fear. Think about it; people who are afraid of heights limit themselves in many ways. Their fear won't allow them to go certain places or do certain things. They are literally paralyzed and confined to only the arenas they aren't afraid of. They cannot fully enjoy life and what it has to offer because their fear keeps them paralyzed. Can you imagine never being able to turn the lights out in your house because you are literally afraid of the dark? Or, what about not being able to ever get on an elevator because of a fear of being trapped in confined spaces? And yet, millions of people suffer from the bondage of phobias every day.

Phobias can be grouped in five categories:

1. Single issue phobias, which involve a single stimulus, such as fear of heights, ladders, insects, animals, enclosed places, etc.

2. Complex phobias, which involve a number of stimuli. With the fear of flying, for example, the person may be afraid of crashing, being enclosed in the plane, losing self-control while on the aircraft, etc.

3. Social phobias, which are a fear of what might occur when in the company of other people. Examples include the fear of blushing, losing self-control, forgetting what you are about to say, fear of trembling, etc.

4. Panic attacks. A panic attack can be a terrifying experience. This is a common phobia and often affects people who normally give the impression of being confident, reliable, and dependable.

5. Agoraphobia, which literally means "fear of the market place." This term once referred to people who were afraid of open spaces, but now it also describes those who experience increasing nervousness with increased traveling distance from their own home. In severe cases they may not venture from home at all.

According to the mental health field, a person is considered to have a phobia if:

- A persistent and intense fear of an object or situation is present, and the fear is felt when even thinking about the situation or object.

- Anxiety begins and intensifies immediately upon being in the situation or seeing the object in question, often developing into a full blown panic attack.

- The individual realizes that the fear and feelings are irrational, yet he or she still has them.

- The individual will do anything to avoid the situation or object he or she is afraid of.

- The anxiety or avoidance begins to severely disrupt the individual's normal day-to-day living and interferes with school, work, and social activities.

A good way to look at phobias is by realizing that they are a magnification of fear on a more intense and specified level. Every fear already has a level of irrationality to it because fear utilizes our imagination to paint a picture of something that has not happened yet. When fear, in its most basic form, shows up in a person's mind, it begins as a thought that works its way down into the emotions if not immediately dealt with and cast out. A phobia is present when the fear becomes concentrated and amplified on a specific issue or object to the point where it becomes all-consuming and completely irrational in its nature.

For example, a person may develop a phobia over something as non-threatening as paper or dust particles. To the average person, being afraid of paper seems ridiculous and even laughable, but to a person who has allowed fear to consume him or her mind in relation to this specific area, contact with paper in any form is very real and frightening. The root issue is the same as any other fear; however, in that it began with a thought that was allowed to take control of a person's mind, will, and emotions.

> "PHOBIAS ARE A PRIME EXAMPLE OF THE BONDAGE THAT IS ATTACHED TO FEAR."

BEYOND WILL POWER

Keep in mind that fear cannot be eradicated simply by exercising will power. Many people attempt to get rid of negative habits by exerting their mental energy; however, will power is not fruitful when dealing with fear. Because it is a spiritual force, it requires spiritual action to overcome. No matter how small or insignificant the fear, it cannot be ignored or "wished" away.

Something like the fear of heights may not seem to be overly intrusive at first, but if allowed to remain in a person's mind and heart, it will eventually create an open door for more fear to come in. There is no such thing as a little fear being okay; it is all bad! Phobias can easily become all-consuming obsessions that steal our joy and rob us of the good life God desires us to live.

One thing that is critical to remember is that everyone can decide whether or not he or she chooses to submit to fear or not. We are not at the mercy of our thoughts, even though it may seem that way sometimes. A person with a phobia is not powerless to take control of his or her mental and emotional health. The gift of free will is wonderful because it means we can take our power back from the enemy and reclaim what he has stolen. In the case of phobias, it would be the peace and soundness of mind described in 2 Timothy 1:7.

Doing everything to control our environments and avoid the object of our fear is not beneficial either because it is still not solving the problem. A person can wash his hands every five minutes in an attempt to avoid germs, but the idea that his actions are helping him actually avoid germs is false. Germs are everywhere, even in the air we breathe. People with phobias falsely believe that by using fear-based control they are helping themselves. The truth is, when we become confined and dictated by our fears, we are in bondage. Making a choice to never get on an elevator or never fly in an airplane will only reinforce the phobia and keep the stronghold of fear intact. We must come out of the prison cell of fear as an act of our will and by our faith if we are to become free of it.

BABY STEPS

Overcoming phobias begins with small steps that progress to full deliverance. Many people live with phobias without needing any treatment, for example, those who fear spiders or heights. However, if a phobia is having a detrimental effect on the social life of the person, he or she may, indeed, need to seek professional counseling. I don't want to discount the importance of receiving psychological therapy, because it can help in some ways. However, even in the midst of treatment by a psychologist or therapist, a person struggling with phobias must incorporate the Word as part of his or her lifestyle in order to overcome the problem. Dealing purely on a psychological level will not result in lasting freedom from the problem.

Treatment of phobias by a therapist will normally involve behavioral therapy, in which a person is gradually exposed to the thing he or she fears in two phases. The first involves confronting the fear, which was discussed earlier in the book as an important way to get rid of it. It is important to stop avoiding the feared situation or object; instead, it needs to be confronted head on.

Because it can be very difficult to start in the midst of the feared situation, the usual approach is by a gradual exposure. This means creating a hierarchy of threatening situations and confronting the least feared situation first before moving on to the more threatening ones. For example, a person with a phobia of spiders might use the following hierarchy as part of his or her exposure:

- Reading about spiders
- Looking at, and then touching, a photograph of a spider
- Looking at/touching a plastic model of a spider
- Looking at/touching a jar with a small spider in it
- Taking the spider out of the jar
- Picking up a large spider.

Clearly, this will be extremely uncomfortable and agitating to the person with the phobia, but it is an important part of dealing with the fear.

To help manage the anxiety that is experienced during the exposure exercises, relaxation and breathing techniques are often used as part of the guided therapy. Therapists will often emphasize the importance of staying in the situation until the anxiety has gone and not trying to escape when the anxiety is high. The objective is to bring the person to a place of sticking out the exposure until the anxiety actually does disappear. Confronting the fear in this way helps the person learn that he or she will survive and can even feel relaxed in the presence of what has been a source of fear for so long.

The second aspect of dealing with phobic fears is to deal with frightening thoughts directly, every time they arise, by replacing them with rational thoughts as well as speaking the Word of God when fear shows up. For example, if a person has a phobia where flying on an airplane is concerned, he may have the thought that says, *"This plane will crash."* The rational thought to counter that thought says, *"I've flown many times before and nothing has happened. Statistically this is the safest way to travel."* On an even deeper level, the application of God's Word as a tool to cast down negative, fearful thoughts is necessary in order to deal with the problem not only from a psychological standpoint but from a spiritual one. While using rational thoughts to counter fear may be relatively effective, only the Word has the power to cast fear out completely. A scriptural response to the aforementioned thought would be, *"My life is redeemed from destruction."* The Word has the spiritual force of God's love behind it, and the power to bring itself to pass. Meditating on the Scriptures will prove to be life-changing and mind-altering for an individual struggling with a phobia. Trusting Jesus can give you the deliverance you seek from any phobia.

GOOD NEWS FOR THOSE WITH PHOBIAS

Isn't it great to know that God has made provisions in His Word for *everything* we will go through in life? There is a scripture for every fear we may face—from the fear of death to the fear of animals. People are cut off from the promises of God because they lack knowledge (Hosea 4:6). This puts the responsibility on us to search the Bible for the answers to our problems and devote our time and effort to filling ourselves with the Word to the point where our mindsets begin to change. Focusing on walking in love toward God and others is the antidote for the fear that comes from self-preservation.

God has given us power, love, and a sound mind, and anything that contradicts these things is to be discarded and cast out of our thinking. Phobias are not the inheritance of Believers. We have the power, through the Holy Spirit and the love of God, to overcome the spirit of fear. Take authority over phobias and face the things you fear with boldness, knowing that God will never leave or forsake you. He will walk you through the process until you achieve total and complete deliverance.

CHAPTER 17
When Will I Get Married?

"Wait on the Lord, and keep his way,
and he shall exalt thee to inherit the land"

(Psalm 37:34).

Have you ever known individuals who were so preoccupied with getting married that they were willing to settle for anyone who showed them some attention? When people have a fear of remaining single, they have a tendency to compromise their standards. Many times, people don't have standards to begin with, which makes things even more complicated. There are many misconceptions concerning the single lifestyle, and as a result, there are those who have gotten off track. The tendency to rush into marriage is particularly strong when there is loneliness and a lack of understanding about what it means to be single and satisfied. Consequently, people end up getting hurt and wasting their time in relationships that were never in God's plan.

Too often, men and women become disillusioned with the single life and spend their mental and emotional energy trying to find "their other half." Some people have the idea that there is a "perfect" person out there for them, and they make locating that person their objective in life. While God does want to bless single people who desire to be married with a spouse, having a fear about remaining single does not bring a mate to you any faster. In fact, the thing you fear will become a reality. Single people must begin to seek God rather than seeking Mr. or Ms. Right. Only when the Lord becomes our priority will the single life become attractive and fulfilling.

WHAT'S THE RUSH?

Why are a lot of people so anxious about getting married? Usually it stems from a sense of loneliness and preconceived notions about what marriage is really like. Some people have a fantasy image of marriage that is based more on the joyful images of the wedding ceremony and honeymoon than on the reality of the marriage covenant and what it entails over the long haul. It is not uncommon for women, in particular, to begin paying attention to all their girlfriends who may be in a relationship or on their way to the altar and question God as to why *they* haven't found their Prince Charming. When allowed to, fear will open the door to competitive jealousy and even depression.

The truth is, many people think marriage is a cure-all for emptiness, loneliness, and a host of other unresolved emotional issues. This belief is nothing more than a myth. If we think everything is going to be fine with us if we get married, it is as if we are saying something is wrong because we are not married. Some people think they are not complete until they find "the one," and that the gaps and obstacles in their lives can only be solved by saying "I do." Unfortunately, marriage is not the answer for loneliness, fear, or an unfulfilled life. The only way to deal with these issues is by developing a relationship with Jesus Christ, not getting into a relationship with another human being who has his or her own issues.

The obsession with marriage is not limited to women, although these emotions tend to be amplified in a lot of women who are single. The truth is, women *and* men can be in a rush to get married, and it almost always sabotages their futures. If you are single and are stressing out about when your time will come, I want you to ask yourself, *What's the rush?* God has a plan for us during every season of our lives, including the single stage. When we maximize this time rather than try to escape it, we will find a new level of love and appreciation for the Lord as we learn to trust Him to meet all our emotional needs, independent of an intimate relationship with the opposite sex. It is actually our discovery of the sustaining power of His love during our season of being single that will make our marriages that much more successful.

WAITING ON THE LORD

There are so many negative connotations attached to the

idea of being single, and they are all based on the idea that something *must* be wrong with you if you reach a certain age or time in your life and have not yet met your husband or wife. Women make statements such as, "My biological clock is ticking," which introduces the fear that if they don't hurry and make something happen with a man, they may actually miss the opportunity to have children. The pressure from family members and even the pressure we put on ourselves to find someone can be overwhelming and unfair. Words such as, "picky," "rigid," and "having issues" are sometimes used to describe people who are and have been single for a significant period of time. It seems like when you are not married, everyone has something to say about the reasons why, whether they are accurate or not. Too often we make marriage an idol, and when this happens, desperation can set in.

I want to let you know that there is absolutely nothing wrong with being single. Everyone has his or her personal standards and ideas about what they are looking for in a mate. The key is to focus on growing in your relationship with God and discovering who you really are during this time in your life. It is not something to run from or be afraid of. Take the pressure off and get to know who you really are before committing your life to someone else.

As always, the Word of God is our reference for making decisions and conducting our lives, including navigating through the season of singleness. Psalm 37:34 in the *Amplified Bible* says something that can definitely apply to the period of time between singleness and married life, "*Wait for and expect the Lord and keep and heed His way, and He will exalt you to inherit the land...*"

Now this idea of waiting on the Lord does not mean sitting around doing nothing. To *wait* on the Lord means to minister to and serve Him; it speaks of being active, not passive. The promise here for those who wait on the Lord is a phenomenal one—they will receive an inheritance. Single people can get busy waiting on the Lord by serving others and finding ways to enhance and increase the Kingdom of God through the gifts God has placed in them. This is a great way to stay focused on the things of God rather than what, or who, isn't in your life.

When I think of inheriting something, I think of something of value. The blessing of God is the empowerment to prosper, and it is available to everyone who is a part of God's family. This blessing is the guarantee of everything promised in the Bible. It is what equips us with the ability to fulfill the will of God for our lives. When we are blessed, nothing is withheld from us that is in God's plan for our lives, which means if we desire a mate, there is no need to become impatient and try to make something happen. Instead, we should focus on the Lord and let the blessing go to work for us. It will seek out and find the person God has for us without us having to interfere. All we have to do is be in position.

God said He would give us the desires of our hearts, and if the desire for a mate is God-given, He will fulfill it. The key is to *wait* upon the Lord, serving Him with all our focus and devotion.

Waiting on the Lord takes the focus off of you and puts it on someone else. This is the essence of walking in love toward God, and walking in love is sure to dispel the fear of not getting married.

UNDERSTANDING TIMING

You have probably heard the phrase, "Timing is everything," and it is true. You can be doing what you are supposed to be doing and trying to make something happen on your own out of fear, and end up disrupting the divine timing of God. When we look at this issue of timing, what comes to mind is the *sequence* that is involved with God bringing our mates to us. In other words, there are certain things that must take place before the next event can unfold in our lives. There is a great danger in being ignorant of the sequence that is involved in God's plan for us. When we don't understand timing, and we allow fear to come on the scene, things are not going to flow smoothly.

Being content in singleness is a foreign concept to a lot of people, because there is this idea that we need to be in an intimate relationship with someone to be truly happy. Now, don't get me wrong, God does not want us to be isolated from others because it is through our relationships that we develop out of selfishness and cultivate the love of God. However, the idea that we need to be involved romantically with someone in order to be happy is simply a distraction the enemy uses to keep people from focusing on their relationship with God. God is madly in love with each and every one of us, whether single or married, and He wants us to realize that it's not about finding your other half; it's about becoming whole in God so you can attract another *whole* individual with just as much to offer as you do.

When I met my wife, I was busy doing the will of God for my life; I wasn't focused on meeting a woman. In fact, when she stepped into a campus Bible study I was teaching, and I noticed her, I fought looking at her because I didn't want to be in lust! However, God made it clear to me that day that there was something special about her that I didn't want to dismiss. We became friends and started dating later on, but I wasn't preoccupied with finding someone because I was lonely. The Lord had plenty for me to do, and as I pursued the will of God, my wife showed up. Not only that, but she fit into God's plan for my life perfectly. Both of us were in the right place, at the right time, doing what we were supposed to be doing. Through a divinely arranged sequence of events, we were able to connect with each other.

Psalm 25:14 in the *Amplified Bible* says something I believe ties into this revelation of becoming satisfied with God only, *before* getting married. It says, *"The secret [of the sweet, satisfying companionship] of the Lord have they who fear (revere and worship) Him, and He will show them His covenant and reveal to them its [deep, inner] meaning."* First, the scripture here says the sweet, satisfying companionship of the Lord is a *secret*. This means it is something that is hidden from people in most cases. The only way to uncover a secret is to search for what is being hidden. The Bible is full of scriptures that talk about *seeking* the Lord and the blessing that comes with the effort we put into it. This is what God wants singles to do rather than getting in fear about when and where their mates will show up.

When we seek the Lord, we will discover that companionship with God is not only sweet but *satisfying*! That may be surprising to some people, but it is the truth. Jesus Christ can satisfy us in ways no human being ever could. He is a friend that sticks closer than a brother, and He knows how to fulfill all of our emotional and spiritual needs. The secrets of the Lord are hidden *for* us, not *from* us.

A lot of singles struggle with areas of their flesh as it relates to sexuality and the fact that they are to remain abstinent until marriage; however, by turning to Jesus Christ through the power of His Word, even the physical desires we have can be kept under subjection to the power of God until the appointed time. The key is to trust and have faith in God and seek Him through His Word and prayer. Cultivating a relationship with Him is the most valuable thing any of us can do.

The second part of the Psalm 25 passage talks about how those who fear, revere, and worship God will be able to partake of this blessed companionship. To fear the Lord simply means to honor and respect Him. We do this by obeying His Word and making it our final authority in life. In doing so, we are able to tap into an immensely gratifying personal relationship with Jesus Christ, enabling us to experience unspeakable joy. It also says that out of this process of seeking, worshiping, honoring and partaking of an intimate relationship with Him, He will reveal His covenant to us. This covenant involves Him exchanging His strengths for our weaknesses, and filling us where we are deficient. With this kind of relationship in our lives, fear, loneliness, and depression simply cannot exist. Gaining a revelation of just how much God wants to be everything we need is what will sustain us when our human emotions try to tell us something different.

SEPARATE, UNIQUE, AND WHOLE

The idea of being single, from God's perspective, is different from what most of us think about when we hear the word. God intends for every unmarried person to be unique and whole in his or her singleness. Adam knew what it was to be single and whole prior to Eve coming on the scene. In Genesis 2:18, God said it was not good for man to be *alone*, so He created suitable help for him. Notice, He did not say it was not good for man to be *single*.

To be separate and unique as a single person means you are different and possess something no one else does, and it also means being conscious of and content with these differences. Have you discovered your uniqueness? Are there things in your life that are challenging your sense of unique identity? If so, where are those ideas coming from? Is there anything you feel is missing or broken in your life? What can you do to discover how to correct those areas? Do you know your calling, purpose, and gifts? Are you maximizing those things for the Kingdom of God? When you begin to look at the single lifestyle, it becomes clear that it is full of things to get busy figuring out and executing. There is plenty to do to be in preparation for the institution of marriage. Singleness is something to be pursued because it highlights your individuality.

Now, the issue with Adam being alone was that he had no one to help him develop into a person who was not self-centered. This is one of the reasons why God created Eve. But outside of Adam being physically alone in the Garden, he didn't lack anything on any level. His aloneness had nothing to do with being lonely or unfulfilled. Adam fellowshipped with God and had perfect communion with Him. The Father visited him regularly in the Garden, and they talked together. Adam was not in fear; in fact, he didn't even know he needed someone else because he was complete as a single person.

God came up with the idea to bring a mate to Adam, not because he was begging and pleading for one, or because he had a desire for a woman, or he was lacking in his emotions. Imagine what would happen if single people everywhere would come to the point of being so preoccupied with their relationship with the Lord that they didn't even realize they were by themselves! That's the type of relationship we should all be striving for with God.

Listen, don't wait to get married to get closer to God; get close to Him now! Don't depend on a relationship with a husband or wife to pursue that type of intimacy. Develop such an intimate relationship with the Lord right now, in your singleness, that you get to the point of enjoying Him every day of your life as if a physical person were by your side. You are not alone!

DISCOVERING YOUR PATH

Isaiah 55:8 says, *"For my thoughts are not your thoughts, neither are your ways my ways, saith the Lord. For as the heavens are higher than the earth, so are my ways higher than your ways, and my thoughts than your thoughts."* If we are going to discover our path in life, which will include the person God has for us, we are going to have to find out God's will and pursue it with passion. The will of God

> **"SINGLE PEOPLE MUST BEGIN TO SEEK GOD RATHER THAN SEEKING MR. OR MS. RIGHT."**

has already been established, it is simply up to us to discover it. We can't do this by trying to discover our husband or wife, but when we begin to pursue the course God has already charted for us, we will find an abundance of blessings along the way, and things will happen without us trying to force the issue.

The question every single person needs to be asking themselves is, "What is the set course for my life? What is that call that God is faithful to bring to fruition in my life? As a single person, discovering who you are is more important than determining who you are supposed to be with. There's a way that seems right to a man, and then there's the way of God, which is free from fear and desperation. Spend time pursuing the path and the mate will show up.

God is a God of plans and purposes, which is why single people have no reason to fear being alone for the rest of their lives. I want to encourage every single person not to be deceived by the lies of the enemy where this issue is concerned. No matter how long you have been single, or what it may look like, God honors those who make Him their first priority in life. Allow Him to reveal Himself as a loving Father, devoted friend, and faithful provider of all our needs. When we allow Him to take control of the reins of our lives, we will find ourselves walking in joy, peace, love, and contentment, which will make fear a thing of the past.

CHAPTER 18
The Fear of Man: The Ultimate Snare

*"The fear of man bringeth a snare: but whoso
putteth his trust in the Lord shall be safe"*

(Proverbs 29:25).

There are so many types of fear that can cause us to become entangled in a yoke of bondage, but one that is particularly common, as well as destructive, is the *fear of man*. Have you ever known someone who was completely consumed with how he or she looked in the eyes of others? So many people are hindered from being all God has called them to be because of what others think of them. Then there are those who are just outright afraid of people. God has created each of us for a specific purpose, and we cannot allow our growth to be stifled by fear. Getting free from people is one of the most liberating things we can do to improve the quality of our lives.

There were many people in the Bible who dealt with the crippling fear of man. For example, the adult generation of the men of Israel who came out of Egypt failed to enter the

Promised Land because they allowed the size and strength of their enemies to intimidate them. The Israelites came to the very edge of the country which God had declared was theirs when He said, *"Go take it, and I will be with you. I will give you the victory."* Before entering the territory they sent out twelve spies to investigate the situation. One of those men was Caleb, who was full of faith and confidence in what God had said.

Caleb wasn't just optimistic about the promise of God; he was emphatic and enthusiastically confident in a positive outcome. The fear of his enemies wasn't even a consideration in his mind. Numbers 13:30 says, *"And Caleb stilled the people before Moses, and said, Let us go up at once, and possess it for we are well able to overcome it."* His report to Moses and the people was, "Let's go do it!" Joshua, one of the other twelve spies, agreed with Caleb, but the rest of the men brought back a different report in verse 31, *"But the men that went up with him said, We be not able to go up against the people; for they are stronger than we."*

These ten men chose to believe what their senses told them about the enemy rather than what God's Word said about them and the obstacles they were facing. Their doubt turned into the fear of people, and it spread like wildfire through the congregation of Israel.

> *And they brought up an evil report of the land which they had searched unto the children of Israel, saying, The land, through which we have gone to search it, is a land that eateth up the inhabitants thereof; and all the people that we saw in it are*

men of a great stature. And there we saw the giants, the sons of Anak, which come of the giants: and we were in our own sight as grasshoppers, and so we were in their sight. And all the congregation lifted up their voice, and cried; and the people wept that night. (Numbers 13:32-14:1).

What happened that day could be likened to the spread of cancer. You see, the fear of people starts when we consider the circumstances rather than what God has said. Those ten spies saw giants rather than the infallible Word of God. Caleb and Joshua on the other hand saw the covenant God made with His people. They had absolute confidence in the Lord, and as a result, those giants looked like grasshoppers to them, not the other way around. Ten spies operated in strong fear, whereas Caleb operated in strong faith.

When we allow ourselves to be intimidated by the outward appearance or manner of other people, we can rob ourselves of what belongs to us according to the Bible. In life, we are going to face situations, circumstances, and *people* who look intimidating. However, we must remain focused on God and the blessing on our lives. Nothing and no one can stop us when our confidence and faith in God are high.

THE LIFE OF SAUL: DEALING WITH THE FEAR OF DISAPPROVAL

Have you ever failed to do something because you were

afraid of what someone else would think of you? Have you ever changed your plans because you feared how someone might respond? Most of us have done these things at one time or another. When we do, we have fallen victim to another form of people bondage.

We can see a classic example of this type of fear in operation in the life of King Saul, who was Israel's first king. Saul was a man who constantly battled insecurity. His was an inner battle rather than one that was confronting him from the outside. The Word says that even though Saul was an extremely tall, attractive man, he was "little" in his own sight (1 Samuel 15:17). His view of himself was marked by an intense inferiority complex and the need to please other people, even at the expense of obeying God. When doubt and fear developed into a fear of people in his life, it cost him and his descendants an entire kingdom.

First Samuel 15:3 gives the account of the Lord's command to Saul to completely destroy his enemies, the Amalekites. God spoke through the prophet Samuel and gave Saul detailed instructions to destroy every living thing associated with these people. *"Now go and smite Amalek, and utterly destroy all that they have, and spare them not; but slay both man and woman, infant and suckling, ox and sheep, camel and ass."*

Now, God's directives may seem extreme, but when it came to preserving the nation of Israel and rooting out any influences of the enemy on His people, there was no room for leniency on the enemy. The sin of the Amalekites was polluting the land and everyone around them. Saul received the directive, but he chose not to obey the Lord because of his fear of what the people would think. 1 Samuel 15:7-9 recounts the story:

And Saul smote the Amalekites from Havilah until thou comest to Shur, that is over against Egypt. And he took Agag the king of the Amalekites alive, and utterly destroyed all the people with the edge of the sword. But Saul and the people spared Agag, and...the lambs, and all that was good, and would not utterly destroy them: but ever thing that was vile and refuse, that they destroyed utterly.

Saul allowed his fear of public opinion and the rationalization of his own mind to distract him from obeying God. This is why fear is so dangerous; it will move us to make decisions that are out of line with God's will. Partial obedience is disobedience and is no better than outright rebellion. In fact, it is actually worse. Saul's failure to trust God and obey him was a great disappointment to both Samuel and the Lord.

Disobedience always hurts those who love us and are counting on us. This is why the fear of man must not be tolerated. There are people who know God has told them to do a particular thing, and they absolutely won't do it because of what people will think. In Saul's case, the situation was made worse because he tried to cover his disobedience with a lie (1 Samuel 15:13). *"And Samuel came to Saul: and Saul said unto him, Blessed be thou of the Lord: I have performed the commandment of the Lord."*

To paint a clearer picture of what happened here, imagine Saul walking up to God's prophet, who already knew what was going on, with a big smile on his face and announcing in his most religious tone, "Verily, verily, my brother, I have obeyed the Lord!" Saul *knew* he had been disobedient! Samuel didn't buy his story, and he questioned him as to why he heard sheep and cattle in the background if, in fact, the spoils of battle had been completely destroyed. The cowardly king replied by placing the blame on the people (1 Samuel 15:14, 15). In reality, his fear of others is what drove *him* to keep what he deemed valuable and destroy what he considered worthy of destruction.

What made the situation worse was when Saul was confronted with his disobedience, instead of confessing and repenting, he became self-righteous. He claimed the best of the animals were spared for a sacrifice to the Lord. However, Samuel informed him that what God wants is not sacrifice but obedience. First Samuel 15:22, 23 says:

> *And Samuel said, Hath the Lord as great delight in burnt offerings and sacrifices, as in obeying the voice of the Lord? Behold, to obey is better than sacrifice, and to hearken than the fat of rams. For rebellion is as the sin of witchcraft, and stubbornness is as iniquity and idolatry. Because thou hast rejected the word of the Lord, he hath also rejected thee from being king.*

Can you see how fearing people can take us on a downward spiral? God knows what's best for us, which means we can trust His instructions, whether they please other people or not.

When we don't check fear at the door, it will build up within us and cause us to lie and compromise in order to protect our own selfishness. That's what happened to Saul. Finally, in 1 Samuel 15:24, the real reason for Saul's disobedience is revealed, *"And Saul said unto Samuel, I have sinned: for I have transgressed the commandment of the Lord, and thy words: because **I feared the people**, and obeyed their voice."*

Saul's insecurities and need for approval caused him to violate the clear command of the Lord God Almighty. He fell into the trap of thinking his position came from pleasing people rather than pleasing God. The result of this was that Saul lost *everything*: his kingship, his anointing, his calling, and finally, his life.

Fear of disapproval is a powerful motivator in the lives of many people today. Some will do practically anything to make sure they have the approval and affirmation of their friends, family members, or co-workers. But the price is too great. Perhaps, like Saul, we have gotten caught up in pleasing people at the expense of God. If so, you know it is a form of bondage. Here are some things people are afraid of where other people are concerned:

- What other people think
- Looking too prosperous
- Appearing too confident

- The way people perceive them

If you have ever dealt with any of these fears, I have some good news for you: *you cannot please people!* There will always be someone who is going to criticize you, no matter what you do. So, you might as well go ahead and please God! Trying to please people won't get your bills paid or help your children. Neither will it get you healed.

I like the Apostle Paul's attitude when it came to dealing with other people's opinions. In Galatians 1:10 he says, *"For do I now persuade men, or God? or do I seek to please men? For if I yet pleased me, I should not be the servant of Christ."* I can identify with Paul's feelings, especially regarding the ministry to which God has called me. Preaching about grace in church is seen as practically blasphemous by many people, Christian and non-Christian. When I discovered the will of God for my life, I couldn't allow what the news media and other people said and thought about grace to affect what I had been commissioned by God to do.

Taffi and I have been through hell and high waters when it comes to being misunderstood and persecuted for preaching the truth of God's Word as it relates to finances also. However, we are committed to the assignment we have been given—to bring revelation and understanding about total life

> "NOTHING AND NO ONE CAN STOP US WHEN OUR CONFIDENCE AND FAITH IN GOD ARE HIGH."

prosperity and the Gospel of grace. We have learned to adopt Paul's attitude in 1 Corinthians 4:3 (The Message), "*It matters very little to me what you think of me, even less where I rank in popular opinion. I don't even rank myself. Comparisons in these matters are pointless.*"

It is futile to be intimidated by the opinions of others; as Paul says, you cannot be a man-pleaser and still wholeheartedly serve Jesus because the root of all man-pleasing is fear. Proverbs 29:25 says the fear of man brings a snare. If we don't get rid of it, we risk missing out on all the victory and success God has planned for us.

THE FEARLESS CHRIST

Jesus is our ultimate example of how to live and operate free from the fear of man. He was fearless in the face of religious persecution, being misunderstood, and constantly having to deal with other people's opinions. Think about it, when Jesus came on the scene preaching about the blessing of God, He was challenging the ideas of the religious leaders of His time. He told people the good news about how the blessing of God could set them free from sin, sickness, and oppression. He spoke of Himself as being one with the Father and that anyone who accepted Him could partake of the covenant of Abraham.

During those times, such ideas were unheard of. Jewish religious culture was deeply ingrained in the hearts and minds of the people. However, Jesus didn't allow *anyone's* opinion of His message to stop Him because He knew His purpose.

Did He suffer for it? Of course He did. Was He persecuted? Tremendously. But at the end of the day, He was able to stand before the Father having completed the redemptive work He was sent to do on the earth.

Jesus finished His course, but that wouldn't have been possible if He had been a people-pleaser. He surrounded Himself with sinners and other people who the Pharisees and Sadducees looked down on. He preached a message of healing and deliverance every day of the week when Mosaic law prohibited it. And yet, many of us who believe in Jesus and the Word of God still allow other people to dictate our actions, attitudes, and pursuits in our everyday lives. It's time to break free. Here are some steps to releasing yourself from people bondage:

1. **Know who you are in Christ.**

    God has not given His people a spirit of fear. That includes the fear of man. We possess the blessing as a result of our relationship with Jesus. Because of this blessing, we are empowered and equipped to do anything God calls us to do. Knowing who we are as Christians is a key to boosting our confidence in every arena of life. There is nothing to fear with the greater One living inside of us.

2. **Allow God to be the source of validation.**

    One of the reasons why people become fearful of what others think is because they are actually searching for validation from sources outside of God. The Bible says we are accepted in the Beloved (Ephesians 1:6). This simply means that if we are in Christ, God accepts us unconditionally. He has already stamped His approval on us, so we do not need to jump through hoops to seek it from others. Walking through life with this type of awareness is liberating.

3. **Remain in God's presence at all times.**

In the presence of God is unconditional love and acceptance—never fear. When we allow ourselves to become caught up in what others may think about us, and we begin to be intimidated by people, it is an indication that we need to get back in God's presence. Psalm 91:1 in the *Amplified Bible* says, "*He who dwells in the secret place of the Most High shall remain stable and fixed under the shadow of the Almighty [Whose power no foe can withstand]. I will say of the Lord, He is my Refuge and my Fortress, my God; on Him I lean and rely, and in Him I [confidently] trust!*" The presence of the Lord provides security, strength, and freedom from fear. It is the answer to the fear of man. God will go before us to ensure we have success in our endeavors; He is our protector and deliverer.

There is no place for fear in the life of a Believer, especially not the fear of people. Fear will rob you of your peace and confidence and place you directly in Satan's path of destruction. If the fear of man has tormented your soul and hindered your progress in life, stand up to it now in the name of Jesus and take authority over it. With our heavenly Father, Jesus, and the Holy Spirit backing you up, there is no reason to be intimidated by anything or anyone in this life!

CHAPTER 19
Keys to Staying Fear-Free

"Beloved, if our heart condemn us, God is greater
than our heart, and knoweth all things"

(1 John 3:21).

The focus of this book is to show you what fear is, the many ways it manifests, and how to get it out of your life. All of us have experienced fear, and some of us have more deeply-rooted fears that must be dealt with in order to walk in victory and receive God's blessings in abundance. Not only do we need to know how to stay free from fear, but we must understand how to keep new fears from developing in our hearts and minds.

We know that fear and torment are a package-deal, which means that if you have one, the other is definitely going to be present. Don't ever fall for the idea that it is okay to have a "little" fear; it is not natural and should *never* be tolerated on any level. Meditating on the Word of God and perfecting God's love in our lives will help us get rid of fear. In addition, the following keys will help us keep fear at bay:

1. **Live right.**

Living according to the Word of God doesn't change God;

it changes us. When we are doing the things we are supposed to do as Christians, we have confidence and boldness. God doesn't want us to avoid sin because He is trying to be mean or diminish our fun in any way. On the contrary, He doesn't want us walking in disobedience because sin opens the door to the enemy in our lives. Satan is out to steal, kill, and destroy us, and when we disobey God's Word we are subject to the curse. We separate ourselves from the blessing of God and become spiritual cowards when we yield to our flesh.

First John 3:21 says, "*Beloved, if our heart condemn us not, then have we confidence toward God.*" A man or woman who is living right does not have to fear anything. When we have confidence before God, it is much easier to stay in faith, which is the only way to effectively activate the law of the spirit of life in Christ Jesus.

I want you to think, for a moment, of a time when you missed the mark. It may have been something only you knew about, or maybe others were involved. Regardless of the circumstances, most likely you had a moment when you felt a sense of condemnation, or that you were unworthy to receive from God.

Praise God for the blood of Jesus that cleanses us from our sins and allows us to boldly come before the Father without guilt or a sense of inferiority. But imagine what people who habitually sin feel like every day of their lives. Most likely it is very difficult for them to receive from God or even believe that He loves them. Remember sin is based in selfishness, and selfishness is based in fear. This is why God wants us to obey Him. Our willingness to yield to His Word will keep us out of fear's grasp.

2. **Speak the Word.**

When fear comes knocking at the door, it is critical that we avoid speaking words that support what the enemy is trying to do in our lives. Agreeing with fear-based thoughts and suggestions and "taking" them by speaking fear-filled words is dangerous because it gives Satan direct authorization to do his will. However, keeping our mouths closed is not enough. We must generate and activate faith by speaking the Word of God with consistency. Regardless of what the circumstances around us are saying, we must never allow them to talk louder than the voice of God.

For example, there may be a bad report circulating at your place of employment about layoffs or cutbacks. Don't join the crowd by panicking and giving voice to the fear of losing your job. Don't start saying things like, "What am I going to do now?" or "How am I going to make it if I get laid off?" Instead,

> "MEDITATING ON THE WORD OF GOD AND PERFECTING GOD'S LOVE IN OUR LIVES WILL HELP US GET RID OF FEAR."

you should immediately open your mouth and say, "I'll not lose my job, praise God! I'm a tither and a giver; therefore, I'm blessed going in and blessed going out. Everything I put my hand to prospers, and my job is not my source; it's my assignment."

When the nightly news reports are full of doom and gloom, where the economy is concerned, don't sit there and entertain that garbage. Turn the television off and keep it off. Find out what the Word says about divine provision and make the Bible your final authority. Allow the good news of the Gospel to be the *only* news you pay attention to on a regular basis.

Speaking the Word rather than the fear-filled thought is the way to attack *any* area where the enemy tries to attack us with fear. We live in a dangerous world in which people are falling victim to their fears at every turn. From finances to personal safety, God has us covered when we trust in Him and speak His Word consistently and constantly. The thing to remember is that we cannot recite the Scriptures one time and expect that to suffice. We must confess what God's Word says about our situations, knowing that God loves us. Do it when you wake up. Do it while you are driving in your car. Repeat it to your spouse and friends.

When we are speaking the Word, all the other thoughts in our minds *have* to stop. It is like a police officer who stands in the middle of the road and blows his whistle for oncoming traffic to stop. Because of the authority invested in his badge, everyone must slow down and come to a halt. Well, the same is true in the realm of the spirit and in the arena of our minds. When we stand up in the middle of circumstances and situations and declare the Word of God with faith and confidence, everything else has to stop and submit to the authority vested in that Word.

I remember a particular occasion before my father had given his life to the Lord. I had been praying for him and witnessing to him for some time. One day I got a phone call.

The voice on the other end of the line said, "Your father has been rushed to the hospital. He has had a heart attack." Immediately, a wave of fear-based panic tried to roll over me, and I felt fear begin to try to wrap itself around my spirit. I heard a voice in my head that said, *Your father is going to die without Jesus and go to hell.* I realized what was happening; the enemy was attacking my mind with fear. That thought didn't come from God, and it certainly didn't come from me.

I got a grip on my emotions and said, "No! It is not his time to go yet. I have prayed and claimed my father for Jesus Christ. I have promises in God's Word that say I can have what I say when I ask in faith. I will settle down right now and stand on God's eternal Word. In the name of Jesus, my father will live and not die. He will recover."

Just as soon as the fear came, it left. I went to the hospital, walked into my father's room, and calmly said hello to him. He asked me how I was doing, and after a long silence he said, "I've decided to get saved." God honored my decision to remain steadfast and immovable from my stance on the Word.

In a crisis situation, it is vital that you recognize instantly that fear is your worst enemy, and you simply can't allow yourself to yield to it. Instead of giving in to it, begin to quote the Word of God. Your confessions will affect your spirit and soul in a tremendous way and build your faith in God.

3. **Stay in the light of God's presence.**

Did you know that fear will cause you to try to hide yourself from the presence of God? That's exactly what happened when

Adam and Eve sinned in the Garden of Eden. Genesis 3:8-10 says:

> *And they heard the voice of the Lord God walking in the garden in the cool of the day: and Adam and his wife hid themselves from the presence of the Lord God amongst the trees of the garden. And the Lord God called unto Adam, and said unto him, Where art thou? And he said, I heard thy voice in the garden, and I was afraid, because I was naked; and I hid myself.*

When we sin, our natural, fleshly reaction is to get into fear and shun the presence of the Lord. The devil will begin to "beat up" on us about how unworthy we are to talk to the Lord or to worship in His house. He will tell us that God is mad at us. The next thing we know, like Adam and Eve, we are hiding out from God in fear, and the enemy is having a field day in our lives.

We cannot fall into this trap! When we miss it, we should simply repent and realize God loves us and has already cleansed us of all sin in Christ. Instead of running from God when we make a mistake, we can move right into the light of His presence and allow Him to set things right again. Allowing fear and condemnation into our hearts will only make matters worse. Practicing the presence of God and dwelling in that presence is a sure way to eliminate fear.

Keep in mind that a fully developed, oppressive spirit of fear does not appear in us overnight; it is cultivated over time, just like faith. If allowed to grow and left unchecked, it will slowly choke the life out of your spirit. Anytime we see fear completely taking over a person's life, remember it didn't start out that way. Fear begins as a seed and eventually develops a root. The soil of the mind is like fertile ground that automatically triggers the process of growth and causes the spirit of fear to overwhelm and overtake our thinking.

What are the seeds of fear? They are thoughts. Fearful thoughts that are allowed to enter our minds, and when given the right conditions, take root, spread, and grow. However, by practicing the three keys discussed in this chapter, we can begin to take back our lives from the clutches of fear. We do not have to be subject to this oppressive spirit any longer when we know how to effectively deal with it. Living a life that agrees with God's Word, making faith-filled confessions, and practicing the presence of God are the ammunition we need to win the fight against fear and eradicate it.

CHAPTER 20
Angels: God's Covenant Enforcers

"For he shall give his angels charge over thee,

to keep thee in all thy ways"

(Psalm 91:11).

Do you believe in angels? If you are a Christian, most likely the answer is yes. But how aware are you of their unique ministry to us? I mentioned angels earlier in this book, but I want to spend more time examining the ministry and assignment of angels to mankind. Though we may know about angels on a surface level, how much time do we actually spend thinking about their presence and work on a daily basis? The extent to which we have faith in angels and know how to get them to work on our behalf is the extent to which we will experience their ministry in our lives on a daily basis. Our confidence in angel power will deliver a death blow to fear.

The Bible has a great deal to say about the ministry of angels, which is why we can be assured that they exist and are available to us. Understanding and appropriating the power of angelic protection is one of the most effective ways to live free from the paralysis and bondage of fear.

Now, you may be wondering, "What do you mean by 'appropriating the power of angelic protection'? I thought angels were just God's messengers." That line of thinking is common, but incorrect. Angels do much more than just deliver messages, although that is a part of what they do. Hebrews 1:13, 14 describes their purpose when it says, *"But to which of the angels said he at any time, Sit on my right hand, until I make thine enemies thy footstool? Are they not all ministering spirits, sent forth to minister for them who shall be heirs of salvation?"* These verses let us know that angels are actually *ministering spirits.*

To whom did the author of Hebrews say angels minister? He said they minister to those who are heirs of salvation. That includes you and me—and all those who are born again. We are heirs according to the promise made to Abraham in Romans 8:17.

> "WE ONLY NEED TO LOOK TO THE WORD OF GOD FOR EVIDENCE THAT THE ANGELS OF GOD ARE LISTENING TO OUR WORDS."

What types of things do angels minister to us? The answer to that question lies in the salvation package. *Salvation* does not only include the born-again experience that takes place when we accept Jesus as Lord and Savior, but it involves much more. The Greek word for salvation is *soteria*, which means "safety, protection, health, healing, deliverance, and soundness." All these things are part of God's covenant, and angels are sent to minister each aspect of salvation to us. They are essentially "covenant enforcers."

WHERE HAVE MY ANGELS BEEN?

You may be wondering why your life has not been the picture of prosperity and abundance if, indeed, you have angels working for you. However, the ministry of angels doesn't just take place in a person's life by chance; it must be accessed by faith, just like any other promise in the Kingdom of God. Healing, financial security, and protection are available to every Beliver, yet only those who stand on God's promises in these areas see results. Well, the same is true where the ministry of angels is concerned.

The truth is that every spiritual benefit promised to us must be activated by faith in order for manifestation to occur. The reason so few people are actually enjoying the service of God's mighty angelic host is that few of us have seen that promise clearly in the Word to have faith in it! In order to build up our faith in angels, we must take a tour of the Scriptures in reference to these powerful beings. When we see it in the Bible, all doubt will be eliminated.

WE'VE BEEN SURROUNDED

In 2 Kings 6, we find a remarkable instance of angelic protection that really speaks of the reality of these unseen ministers. In this biblical account, the king of Syria was tired of the prophet Elisha knowing about his battle plans and telling the king of Israel beforehand. The Lord told Elisha what the king was planning to do even before his generals did! As a result, the king sent his most ruthless troops to find and kill Elisha.

One morning, Elisha and his servant Gehazi woke up to find themselves surrounded by Syrian troops (2 Kings 6:15):

> *And when the servant of the man of God was risen early, and gone forth, behold, an host compassed the city both with horses and chariots. And his servant said unto him, Alas, my master! How shall we do?*

Understandably, Gehazi was disturbed. From what he could see in the natural realm, it appeared as if he and his master were going to die. Have you ever been in a situation where it looked as if you were "surrounded" by circumstances and situations that threatened to steal your peace, destroy your life, and set you back? Has it ever looked hopeless for you? Regardless of the situation, all of us have encountered pressure that comes from the enemy and that requires faith to overcome.

Despite how bleak the situation looked, Elisha was not bothered at all by what was going on around them. In fact, his response didn't make sense to Gehazi at all, "*And he answered, Fear not: for they that be with us are more than they that be with them*" (2 Kings 6:16). In other words, Elisha was saying, "Relax, Gehazi, we have them outnumbered."

At this point, the servant probably thought his man of God had lost his mind! It was obvious to him that there were only two of them and hundreds of enemy troops. Why did one of these two men respond with fear and the other with calm assurance? The difference between their outlooks on the situation was that Elisha understood his covenant with God through Abraham, which included the ministry of angels. Elisha knew that the God he served would protect him and deliver him from the hand of the enemy.

Understanding the strength of God's covenant gives us peace, even in the most desperate circumstances. Additionally, when we are covenant-minded, we can see with spiritual eyes.

> *And Elisha prayed, and said, Lord, I pray thee, open his eyes, that he may see. And the Lord opened the eyes of the young man; and he saw: and, behold, the mountain was full of horses and chariots of fire round about Elisha* (2 Kings 6:17).

Suddenly, Gehazi became aware of what Elisha had known all along: When we are in covenant with the Most High God, His angels surround us with protection 24 hours a day. Like Elisha, we are surrounded by protecting angels right now! And, just as with the prophet, they are waiting for our words of confidence and faith—words that are consistent with the blood covenant with God that we have through Jesus Christ—so they can go into action.

When fear tries to raise its ugly head and intimidate us through circumstances, situations, and even wicked people, we need to have our spiritual eyes opened to the truth of what is in our presence. No matter how many enemies the devil sends against us, there are more for us than there are against us. Our enemies are completely outnumbered!

So how do we put our angels to work? We do so by declaring our covenant and speaking the promises of God in faith. Some people may say, "If I could see angels, then I would believe." However, Jesus says that we are blessed when we don't see and still believe (John 20:29). While God may allow us to see an angel in our lifetime, we should never rely on what we can see and perceive with our senses to dictate whether we believe or not. We must see our angels through the eyes of faith. They are present because God says they are there. That's what real Bible-faith is all about.

SEE THEM AS THE PROMISE POLICE

Fear is a direct assault on the promises of God and the core of security He wants us to personally experience through His covenant. Angels are part of God's covenant plan to protect and serve His people. Galatians 3:19 says something very interesting in this regard, "*Wherefore then serveth the law? It was added because of transgressions, till the seed should come to whom the promise was made; and it was ordained by angels in the hand of a mediator.*"

The aspect of this verse I want to focus on is that the law was *ordained by angels.* Another way of translating that is to say the law was "put into effect" by angels. According to this scripture, we see that one of the functions of angels is "to put into effect" the promises of the covenant. In other words, angels are our "covenant-enforcers."

Policeman sometimes say, "I don't make the laws; I just enforce them." Well, that is precisely the role of angels. They are spiritual "policemen" who carry out the covenant provision of protection, among other things. They only do this, however, if we release them to execute their divine assignments. How do we loose our angels? We speak God's Word. The Bible says angels hearken unto the *voice* of the Word of God, so when we speak the Scriptures, they go into action to enforce them.

For example, fear may be trying to attack you in the area of physical health and healing. If you don't know what the Word says about healing, you won't be able to release your angels to work on your behalf. But when you know the Word, which says that by the stripes of Jesus Christ we were healed (1 Peter 2:24), you will have the exact words you need to command your angels to bring that scripture to pass. They will spring into action to do what is necessary in the spirit realm to bring healing to you. Why? They have no choice but to enforce the terms of God's covenant.

GOD'S COVENANT OF PROMISE

Everything we have faith to see manifest in our lives goes back to the covenant God made with us through Abraham. This covenant is many-faceted; it contains promises of eternal life, healing, provision, and much more. Armed with this knowledge, there is absolutely no way fear can get the upper hand in our lives.

One of the most exciting and reassuring parts of the covenant we have with God is His promise of protection. Psalm 91 is one of the most powerful and all-encompassing passages of Scripture because it covers so many areas in which fear tries to attack. From start to finish, this psalm declares God's covering of protection and safety over every Believer, which is why we have nothing to fear in this world. Verses 11 and 12 specifically talk about the role angels play in bringing the terms of the covenant of protection to pass. It says angels have *charge* over us, meaning they are assigned to us and will keep us in *all* our ways.

No matter where you are or where you go, you are surrounded by an invisible force-field of angelic protection, which should be quite comforting. No matter what may come against you or what is going on around you, the truth of God's Word is a refuge from Satan. Building an awareness of angels into your consciousness is an important key to living a fear-free life.

ANGELS ARE NO LONGER HINDERED

When the subject of angels is discussed, the incident in the book of Daniel is usually brought up, where an angel was hindered by a demonic principality. Some people may wonder whether or not our angels can be held up in a similar manner as well. Before we answer that question, let's look at that particular passage for clarification.

> In those days I Daniel was mourning three full weeks. I ate no pleasant bread, neither came flesh nor wine in my mouth, neither did I anoint myself at all, till three whole weeks were fulfilled. And in the four and twentieth day of the first month, as I was by the side of the great river, which is Hiddekel; Then I lifted up mine eyes, and looked, and behold a certain man clothed in linen, whose loins were girded with fine

gold of Uphaz: His body was like the beryl, and his face as the appearance of lightening, and his eyes as lamps of fire, and his arms and his feet like in colour to polished brass, and the voice of his words like the voice of a multitude (Daniel 10:2-6).

This passage is describing a vision of an angel that Daniel received after three weeks of fasting, praying, and waiting for an answer from God. He finally experienced a breakthrough when the angel made his appearance. In verses 12 and 13, the angel explains to Daniel that his prayer was heard by God from the very beginning, but he was delayed by the presence of a demonic principality that fought him for 21 days.

Can demonic powers hinder the angels of God like that now? The answer is no! Satan was stripped of his authority in the spirit realm when Jesus defeated him. Colossians 2:15 says, *"And having spoiled principalities and powers, he made a shew of them openly, triumphing over them in it."* And 1 Peter 3:22 says, *"Who is gone into heaven, and is on the right hand of God; angels and authorities and powers being made subject unto him."*

Things are different now that Jesus has taken his seat at the right hand of the Father. All authority in heaven and on earth has been given to Jesus, and as joint-heirs with Him, we also have authority to command things on earth and in heaven. When we loose our angels in the authority of the name of Jesus Christ, they operate unhindered and unchallenged for those who speak God's words of promise.

OUR WORDS ARE CRITICAL

We only need to look to the Word of God for evidence that the angels of God are listening to our words. Luke 12:8, 9 says, *"Also I say unto you, Whosoever shall confess me before men, him shall the Son of man also confess before the angels of God: But he that denieth me before men shall be denied before the angels of God."* Whether we believe it or not, our words are being heard by an audience of angels. Revelation 5:11 says the number of angels that surround the throne of God is *ten thousand times ten thousand, and thousands of thousands.* To sum those numbers up, it basically is around a trillion angels, which means ten thousand angels for every man, woman, and child alive on the earth today!

The bottom line here is that there is no shortage of angel power to put to work on our behalf. If as much as half the earth's population became born again, there would still be 20,000 angels at each believer's disposal to carry out and enforce their covenant with God. Imagine 20,000 servants "on the mark, set, and ready to go" on your behalf!

As we can see, there is a mighty host of angels waiting to hear the Word of God come out of a Believer's mouth. Psalm 103:20 says angels *hearken* unto the voice of the Word. To *hearken* means to "listen for, to pay close attention to, and to hear and do." Angels are listening for the voice of God's Word. Give the Word voice, and they will respond.

When you have bills that need to be paid and the fear of lack tries to creep into your mind, speak the Word. Make confessions that declare what God has already said about the situation. The Word is the ignition switch that turns on angelic activity. When they hear the Word coming out of your mouth, they begin moving and influencing in the spirit realm to make God's covenant promises a reality in your life.

On the other hand, when you speak negative words of fear, you take your angels out of the picture. Those kinds of words do not align with what God's covenant says about your situation. In the presence of doubt, fear, and unbelief, angels have no choice but to bow their heads, fold their hands, and wait for you to change your confession.

NO FEAR HERE

There is no place for fear in the life of a Believer. The spirit of fear will rob us of everything that is good about the Christian life here on the earth. It will steal our peace and torment our souls. But that isn't even the worst part.

The most devastating part of fear is that it connects you to everything you don't want to happen to you. As we have discussed throughout this book, it is time to get rid of all fear by changing the way we talk, getting a revelation of the angels of God, using our imagination to see ourselves walking in God's promises, and acting in faith. When we do these things, the spirit of fear will be uprooted from our lives, and we will begin walking in the blessings, power, and peace that are rightfully ours.

CHAPTER 21
Plead the Blood

"And there are three that bear witness in earth,
the spirit, and the water, and the blood:
and these three agree in one"

(1 John 5:7).

If you have ever seen the movie *Superman,* you know that the one thing that absolutely incapacitated Superman was kryptonite. This element rendered an otherwise invulnerable hero completely helpless. As Believers, we have something at our disposal that has the same debilitating effect on our enemy. This fear-antidote cannot be overlooked because it is probably the most powerful component of God's covenant with us. It is the blood of Jesus, and when we know and understand its power, we can live in absolute dominance over the devil and the spirit of fear in all of its forms. The blood of Jesus is an invaluable tool in our spiritual arsenal because it is a constant reminder to Satan of his eternal defeat. Pleading the blood over the areas of our lives that fear tries to infiltrate renders Satan helpless, and is vital to our victory.

First, as Believers, we must understand that we are empowered by the blood of Jesus, and it is a spiritual weapon against the spirit of fear. However, in order to reap the full benefits of the blood of Jesus, we must have faith in it. Faith in the blood is knowing what it has accomplished and knowing the provisions that have been made available to us through it. One of those provisions is divine protection and deliverance from anything we are afraid of. Remember, fear is having faith in that thing's ability to harm you. But when we focus on developing faith in the blood of Jesus, we become spiritual giants that are able to live completely fear-free lives.

The enemy will always attack us if we are ignorant about the blood of Jesus and how powerful it is. This is a topic many Believers have been in the dark about. Sure, we've heard sermons on the blood, and know how to use the term as a religious cliché, but most people do not have a working revelation of the blood of Jesus and what it means for them on a daily basis.

Listen, we do not have to be subject to the spirit of fear! This goes against the predominant view of the world, which is full of fear and subscribes to it as if nothing can be done to stop it. But for those who put their hope and trust in the Lord, fear doesn't have to dominate us.

BENEFITS OF THE BLOOD

We know that one of the keys to staying free from fear is to remain in the light of God's presence at all times. Think about it, if we stay in the presence of God, the enemy can't touch us.

The blood of Jesus plays an important role in us being able to do this because it is through and by His blood that we have a right to even enter into the Father's presence. Without the blood, we would be locked out of the presence of God and cut off from everything His presence affords us, such as peace, protection, deliverance, and strength.

Hebrews 10:19-22 says, "*Having therefore, brethren, boldness to enter into the holiest by the blood of Jesus... Let us draw near with a true heart in full assurance of faith, having our hearts sprinkled from an evil conscience, and our bodies washed with pure water.*" It is only through the blood of Jesus that we are able to draw close to the Father, and, according to Psalm 91:1, the secret place of the Most High is where protection and peace are. The blood is our access key to Him. God honors the blood because He honors His Son. When we are in Christ, we are "blood-washed," and God sees us through the eyes of Jesus.

We know that fear is Satan's attempt to assault our peace and move us into a place of being emotionally-ruled. But maintaining confidence in the blood of Jesus will lift us above any attack of the enemy. Why is it so powerful? It is the only thing that brings us into right standing with the Father. Jesus was the perfect sacrifice because He never sinned. He was *made* sin so we could *become* righteous. God cut a covenant with us through the blood sacrifice of Jesus on the cross, and we have been redeemed from everything that came with the curse, including fear. His blood is the only thing that gives us that level of freedom and security.

As with anything in the Kingdom of God and the Word, trust is an essential part of reaping the benefits of the blood of Jesus. In fact, the level of trust we are willing to release in the blood will be the level of results we get in our lives where deliverance from fear is concerned. We must become immovable and unshakeable in our commitment to trust in the blood of Jesus.

Another reason the blood is such an effective antidote against fear is because it cleanses us from all sin. Sin is based in fear, and when we have not dealt with sin in our lives, fear and selfishness are going to be present; however, the blood of Jesus is the only thing that has the power to completely cleanse us from sin (1 John 1:7). This cleansing gives us the confidence to boldly come before the Father again and again, without a sense of guilt, fear, or condemnation.

TAPPING INTO THE BLOOD'S ABILITY

Now, it is important that we know exactly what the blood does. It carries specific abilities that will ensure freedom from fear when applied to our lives. Let's examine them more closely.

1. **The blood releases us from every stronghold of the devil.**
   A stronghold is a house made of thoughts that is nourished and maintained by the enemy. Many times we allow strongholds to develop in our lives because of thoughts we don't cast down with God's Word. Once a stronghold has developed, the enemy has authority in that area. However, through the blood of Jesus, we can get rid of the things that hold us captive.

At the root of every stronghold is some level of fear, which is why the blood is so necessary. By applying the blood to every area in which the enemy is holding ground, we release the power of God to begin infiltrating those places. And when we do this, while walking in the light of God's Word, fear is rooted out.

2. **The blood protects us from the onslaughts of the devil.**

    When it comes to protection, the blood of Jesus gets the job done, hands down. We can begin appropriating the protective power of the blood by declaring it out loud every day over our families, homes, finances, health, and anything else that concerns us. When the enemy comes against your mind with fear, release the power of the blood of Jesus with words of faith. Jesus has reconciled us back to Himself through the blood, which means we are under His protection and care (Colossians 1:20).

3. **The blood of Jesus gives absolute victory in the midst of a storm.**

    All of us have encountered times of testing and trial, and will continue to do so as we walk out our faith as Believers. It is during these times that the enemy will attack us with fear, particularly the fear that what the Word says will not come to pass in our lives. He tries to attack our confidence in God and get us to doubt Him by having us focus on our circumstances rather than the promises of God. However, the blood of Jesus guarantees our victory, no matter what we are facing. Jesus already paid the price for us to be able to win over every trial and test. He conquered death, hell, and the grave so that we would be able to win in life.

4. **The blood of Jesus has the power to give us complete breakthrough in prayer.**

I have often said that every success, or failure, in life is a prayer failure. Prayer is the key to winning in life's endeavors, which is why Christians must make it an integral part of their daily routines. But what makes prayer the link to our success? The blood! The blood enables us to boldly approach the Father, enter into His presence, and get answers to our prayers. We have a blood-bought right to receive the things we desire and ask for in our prayer time, when those things are in line with the Word of God. When I pray, I plead the blood of Jesus over my prayer time and declare the power of the blood over every area of my life. I bring before God every issue, concern, and request, and I petition Him through and by the blood of Jesus. We do not have to be afraid that God won't answer our prayers when we get the blood in on the situation.

5. **The blood releases, for our enjoyment, all the benefits of salvation.**

There are a lot of things included in the salvation package besides what I call "fire insurance" or deliverance from hell after we die. Salvation includes everything good promised in the Word. The covenant of God includes protection, peace, preservation, and wholeness across the board; God left no area uncovered when He sent Jesus to die for us.

Therefore, we have access to a multitude of benefits that are designed to improve the quality of our lives.

Unfortunately, many Christians go through their entire lives without tasting the goodness of the Lord in its fullness. Too often, we live far below the standard God intends for us and accept a way of life that doesn't even come close to God's plan for our lives. In order to begin to see the benefits of salvation, we have to release our faith in the blood of Jesus. The covenant was ratified through His blood, which is why it is an essential part of the salvation equation.

RECEIVE IT!

The things of God (and the things Satan wants to introduce to us) become a reality in our lives when we receive them. Titus 2:14 says, "*Who gave himself for us, that he might redeem us from all iniquity, and purify unto himself a peculiar people, zealous of good works.*" The blood of Jesus has already accomplished everything we need to be successful and victorious. We have been redeemed from sin, darkness, sickness, and poverty already, so there is no reason to fear any of these things! Our part is to simply receive, by faith, what the blood has done.

> "WHEN IT COMES TO PROTECTION, THE BLOOD OF JESUS GETS THE JOB DONE, HANDS DOWN."

We develop our trust in the blood of Jesus by studying it in the Word and meditating on it all the time. The times in which we live are dangerous, to say the least, but with our confidence in the right place, we don't have anything to worry about.

We understand that we receive the promises of God by believing in our hearts and speaking those things out loud as an act of our faith. The same is true where the blood of Jesus is concerned. We must get our mouths involved with the process in order to counter any fear the enemy pressures us with and activate the power of the blood. Every day we must confess what the blood has done for us and cover all areas of our lives with it by making certain declarations such as:

- I cover my mind and thoughts with the blood of Jesus.
- I cover my doorpost and possessions with the blood of Jesus (Exodus 12:13).
- I overcome the devil through the blood of Jesus (Revelation 12:11).
- I am made perfect through the blood of the everlasting covenant (Hebrews 13:20, 21).
- I have boldness to enter into the presence of God through the blood (Hebrews 10:19).
- I have redemption through the blood of Jesus, and I am redeemed from the power of evil (Ephesians 1:7).
- I rebuke all spirits of torment and fear because I have peace through the blood of Jesus (Matthew 26:28).
- I receive healing and health through the blood of Jesus.
- The blood of Jesus bears witness to my deliverance and salvation (1 John 5:8).
- The blood of Jesus cleanses me from all sin (1 John 1:7).

- Jesus resisted unto blood, and His blood gives me victory (Hebrews 12:4).
- I rebuke Satan, the accuser of the brethren, through the blood of Jesus (Revelation 12:10).

Incorporating these confessions into your daily prayer time is an effective way to combat the enemy when he attacks you with fear. The voice of God's Word will send angels into action, to carry out everything you speak.

Now, more than ever, we must utilize the tools God has made available to us in order to triumph over Satan. He will constantly try to use fear as bait to move us out of the will of God for our lives. However, by developing confidence in the blood of Jesus, we can defeat him every time. It is the key to our victory, so use it. The only one running in fear will be the devil!

CHAPTER 22
The Truth about the Fear of the Lord

"The fear of the Lord is the beginning of wisdom: and the
knowledge of the holy is understanding"
(Proverbs 9:10).

The term "fear God" is a common source of confusion among Christian as well as non-Christian. In fact, not having understanding about what it means to fear the Lord can result in a warped view of God that drives us away from Him, rather than toward Him. When the Word talks about fearing God, it is not saying we are to be afraid of Him in the sense that He is a mean taskmaster waiting to strike us down when we make mistakes. This fear comes from the devil, and it brings torment with it. However, to fear God means to honor and respect Him in every decision we make. When we fear the Lord, we have a reverence for Him that moves us to obey His Word.

God didn't give us commandments because He is trying to make our lives miserable. His concern for us is birthed out of love and a desire for us to experience the very best in life. Unfortunately, the society in which we live doesn't value God or His commandment of love because it is viewed as bondage. People want to live selfish lives that disregard the Bible, and anything that is perceived as a threat to their selfish lifestyle is rejected. However, the commandments of God were never designed to make us unhappy, but to protect us and give us life.

> "WHEN WE FEAR THE LORD, WE HAVE A REVERENCE FOR HIM THAT MOVES US TO OBEY HIS WORD."

So what does it mean to walk in the fear of God? It simply means to respect, honor, and live a worshipful life before God. First John 5:2, 3 says something so powerful, "*By this we know that we love the children of God, when we love God, and keep his commandments. For this is the love of God, that we keep his commandments: and his commandments are not grievous.*"

Our love for God is evident when we are willing to be led by His love for us. Whether it deals with our finances (tithing and giving offerings), embracing holiness and sexual purity, or even our prayer lives, the fear of God must be what drives us to do what we do as Believers.

THE WISDOM CONNECTION

Proverbs 9:10 says something interesting about the connection between the fear of the Lord and wisdom, "*The fear of the Lord is the beginning of wisdom: and the knowledge of the holy is understanding.*" Proverbs 4:7 says wisdom is the principle thing and understanding is of the utmost importance. When we put it all together, it becomes clear that wisdom starts by having a reverence and respect for God. When we honor Him and make His Word our final authority in life, we open the door to the wisdom of God, which is critical to our success.

There are so many benefits to walking in the fear of God, which is why this important aspect of our relationship with the Father must be examined. One reason people shun the commandment of love is because they don't know or understand the benefits of having faith in God's love for us. Unfortunately, much of the body of Christ continues to go to church and do all the religious things that Christians are supposed to do, but they lack one thing: results. When genuine confidence in God's love for us and true honor for Him are not present and motivating our actions, the things we do in the name of Christianity won't yield anything.

Besides being the doorway to the wisdom of God, Psalm 34:7-9 gives some of the benefits of having godly reverence, or fear. It says, *"The angel of the Lord encampeth round about them that fear him, and delivereth him. O fear the Lord, ye his saints: for there is no want to them that fear him."* Again, when we see the word *fear* here, it is not talking about being afraid of God because He is mean, harsh, or wants to hurt and punish us. God is love (1 John 4:16) and He only wants the best for us.

The benefits of honoring God are well worth it. In this passage of scripture, the first thing we see related to fearing God is divine protection. Divine angelic protection is a guarantee for those who keep God first place in their lives. He promises to deliver us when we fear Him. I know firsthand about the delivering power of God. Several years ago, I was in a near fatal car accident, and I actually saw angels break through the natural realm to assist me. Divine deliverance from all manner of danger is available to us when we reverence the Lord.

Secondly, we see that fearing God brings with it provision. He says we will have no wants when we fear Him. I don't know about you, but that sounds like an awesome promise to me. Going through life without want or lack of any kind is a blessing that I definitely want to experience. God is a Father, and like any father who receives respect from His children, He is prompted to do even more for us when we honor Him.

THE FEAR OF THE LORD IN OUR RELATIONSHIPS

This idea of reverencing God goes beyond our one-on-one relationship with Him and extends to how we relate to one another. God is all about relationships, and how we interact with and treat others is equally important to Him.

Ephesians 5 discusses the connection between the family and the church and instructs us to submit to one another in the fear of God (vv. 21). This is a particularly important command to remember in marriages. Many times, one spouse will use the concept of submission in a one-sided way in order to control or manipulate the other, but God says we are to submit to *each other* as an act of our honor and reverence for Him. This makes the concept of submission less about us and more about God.

A wife who wants to walk in the fear of the Lord in her marriage will obey the Word out of respect for God, Who says, "*Wives, submit yourselves unto your own husbands, as unto the Lord.*" (Ephesians 5:22). And husbands who fear God will obey the command to love their wives as Christ loves the church (vv. 25). In addition, children are to obey their parents, and employees are to submit to their employers and work "as unto the Lord." Everything we do must have the motive of wanting to honor God, and we do this by following His instructions to us.

The truth is, most of us have learned how to operate in the fear of the Lord in church, but when it comes to how we treat others, we tend to forget how important it is to maintain the same attitude of reverence for God. When everything we do becomes about honoring God, we will truly begin to experience the blessing that comes from it. Making changes according to the Word, where our relationships are concerned and walking in the fear of the Lord, go hand in hand.

The Bible says the person who will live in the fear of the Lord will have great peace. There are so many people trying to find peace in things outside of God, but according to Psalm 128:1-6, the satisfaction many of us are looking for is only found by submitting to and honoring God. The person who is living and walking in the fear of the Lord is going to be whole in every area of their lives. Nothing will be missing, lacking, or broken— spirit, soul, body, family, or finances. This is not to say we will not go through tough times where our faith will be tested, but at the end of the day the person who fears and reverences God will be experiencing a level of fulfillment unknown to the person who chooses not to receive God's love and honor and worship Him.

REVERENCE FOR GOD EMPOWERS US

I believe that we are living in a time when God desires to give great wisdom to those who are in the body of Christ. He is ready to show us things we have never seen before. The Lord knows all the answers to every question and problem we may be facing in life, and He has a million ways to get us to our final destination of total life prosperity. All we need is just one of them. He is ready to reveal Himself to us and give us the things we are seeking Him for, but He is looking for people who will be loyal to Him.

Psalm 128:1 says, *"Blessed is every one that feareth the Lord; that walketh in his ways."* This is the key to our victory. When we walk in His ways out of respect and honor, we are empowered to prosper! Living this way is for our good, and will keep us from the fear and torment that Satan wants to bring into our lives.

The more time we spend reading and meditating on His Word, the more knowledgeable we will become about what it means to walk in God's ways. If you desire to be a Christian who pleases God, become a person who holds the Word of God in the highest esteem. God takes pleasure in those who fear Him and will deliver on every promise He has made. The fear of the Lord is not a bad thing. It will release the blessing like never before. Examine your life to determine if you truly are honoring God in your thoughts, words, and actions. Renewing our minds in this area will make the difference in our lives.

CHAPTER 23
How to Overcome Agitation

*"Peace I leave with you, my peace I give unto you: not
as the world giveth, give I unto you. Let not your heart
be troubled, neither let it be afraid"*

(John 14:27).

Have you ever been on a boat ride? One thing every boat
will have on hand is an anchor. This valuable tool enables the
boat to remain stable in one spot if the sailor decides he wants
the boat to stop moving for whatever reason. Once that anchor
is released deep in the water, it provides support and stability,
even in the midst of a storm. The anchor is a fitting metaphor
for the role the Word of God should play in every Christian's life.
It is what keeps us from being tossed around by the storms of
life, and it keeps us stable when we are tempted to quit on God.
Agitation is one of those storms that the enemy will use against
us in order to disturb our peace. However, by maintaining an
unwavering stand on God's Word, our peace will remain intact.

The Bible says Jesus has given us His peace (John 14:27), and
yet there are many things that challenge this peace every day.

These things are designed by Satan to keep us from resting in the Lord. Agitation is an emotion that has the potential to distract us and move us away from God's will for our lives. The Word actually groups agitation with other emotions, such as being troubled and fearful. Since this is the case, we can conclude that agitation is another face of fear that tries to show itself in our lives. Therefore, we must be able to recognize it and resist it.

In the Amplified Bible, John 14:27 reads, "*Peace I leave with you; my [own] peace I now give and bequeath you.*" To *bequeath* something means to personally hand it down to someone. When Jesus says He has bequeathed something to us, it means He has personally handed it down to us! He has literally bestowed the very same peace He possesses, the same peace that exists in the Father, to us. This is the same peace that kept Jesus from being moved by trouble and irritation during His time on the earth. It is the peace that kept Him from quitting on God when He was facing the agony of the crucifixion. Jesus' peace is a supernatural peace that supersedes anything we find in the world, and every Christian can walk in it if he or she receives it by faith.

CHOOSING GOD'S WORD

Agitation is specifically designed to disrupt our peace and get us in a place where we doubt God's ability to handle the situations we face. In order to keep from being agitated, we must choose God's Word and make it the final authority over our emotions, no matter what is going on. Sometimes it feels as if we can't avoid getting irritated about something someone has said or done, but that simply isn't true. *We* make a choice to become agitated, troubled, disturbed, or afraid, just like we make a choice to remain focused on God's Word. In fact, the moment we make a decision to let God's Word govern our lives, Satan tries to change our minds by working through situations, circumstances, and people to cause extreme emotional disturbances. But we must determine in our minds to refuse agitation when it shows up.

There is a progression that takes place when we become agitated. When we are disturbed and irritated about something, we tend to become fearful. For example, a husband and wife may have a financial disagreement because of one spouse's overspending. The irritated spouse, who allows agitation to gain a foothold in his or her mind, will find fear trying to creep into the area of finances in the home. The issue may have been that the wife or husband miscalculated how much money was in their checking account before making a purchase that sent the account into overdraft, or someone may have used a credit card for an unnecessary purchase. This progresses into operating in fear of lack where finances are concerned. And when fear is present, Satan has an open door through which he can enter our lives and bring to pass the things we fear.

When we become agitated, we walk away from our peace and become afraid that the source of our peace—God—has failed us. We must understand that this is part of the enemy's plan.

The key to maintaining our peace is to keep our minds on the Word of God. Isaiah 26:3-4, in the *Amplified Bible*, reads: *"You will guard him and keep him in perfect and constant peace whose mind [both its inclination and its character] is stayed on you, because he commits himself to you, leans on you, and hopes confidently in you. So trust in the Lord (commit yourself to Him, lean on Him, hope confidently in Him) forever; for the Lord God is an everlasting Rock [the Rock of Ages]."*

There are several key things to be aware of in this passage as it relates to God's promise of peace. First, we must keep our minds stayed on Him as an act of our will. This is often the biggest challenge when agitation rears its ugly head because the tendency is to let the situation be an excuse to get agitated. However, those moments are tests to see how we handle our emotions. We have two choices: to submit to agitation and end up doing or saying something that does not align with God's Word, or to submit to God's Word and command our minds to maintain godly focus. The wonderful promise we have is that not only will God keep us in peace, but it will be *perfect* peace that is constant, which means it never ends. Isn't it exciting to know there is a continual stream of peace available to us when we refuse to take our eyes off God's Word?

The latter part of the scripture deals with trust. When we keep our minds stayed on God, it is an expression of our trust in Him and His ability to take care of whatever situation we are up against. Trust is different from faith, in that faith is confidence while trust is commitment. It is like a mountain that cannot be moved (Psalm 125:1).

Joseph's life was the epitome of trust in God. He had plenty of things to get agitated about on his way to his destiny. He was rejected by his brothers and sold into slavery by them, but these things did not destroy his trust in God. He was falsely accused of sexual harassment and thrown in jail, but he never stopped trusting in the Lord. Joseph overcame each challenge in his life by trusting God. He did not know he was about to be promoted to a position of authority, over the entire land of Egypt, when he was in the midst of these agitating challenges, but he continued to maintain a conquering mentality. As a result, he entered God's rest. Similarly, when we enter God's rest, negative situations will not have the power to agitate us.

Our trust in God is demonstrated when we commit ourselves to Him, lean on Him, and hope confidently in Him. We do this by always keeping the Word before our eyes and in our ears, and declaring it by making confessions of faith. On the other hand, agitation dilutes our trust in God and His Word, which is why we must not let it get the upper hand.

Keep in mind that we open the door to fear when we lean on our own understanding instead of what the Word says. This gives place to agitation. We can cut off fear and dismantle agitation by constantly meditating on the Word of God *before* agitation shows up. The Word that is alive and active within us acts like a buffer against the enemy's attacks on our minds and emotions.

A SIGN OF YOUR BREAKTHROUGH

Attacks from the enemy don't happen without a reason. Satan has a specific goal in mind. He can only work through the avenue of our emotions and thoughts, so he wants to stir people up and create situations that cause us to be irritated. He knows that when we get agitated, we are more likely to say something that does not line up with God's Word, and will short-circuit the wonderful blessings God has planned for us.

It is not uncommon for highly agitating situations to show up right before a major breakthrough takes place in our lives. In fact, we can definitely prepare for a breakthrough when the enemy starts using agitation against us. Here are some things to remember when we see a storm of agitation brewing:

1. We do not have to be afraid while standing on the Word of God. He will not allow us to be put to shame (Isaiah 54:2-4).

2. God has a covenant of peace with us, and He will not break it. This is our heritage (Isaiah 54:10-17).

3. No weapon formed against us will work when the Word is our foundation and we continue to speak it. Every tongue that rises up against us will be condemned by our declaration of the scriptures.

Another antidote for agitation, which stops the devil in his tracks, is thanksgiving. Instead of allowing ourselves to be troubled by what we see, we can choose to have an attitude of gratitude, by faith. When we give thanks, we are focusing on the good things God has done for us. In fact, agitating situations can be used as opportunities to cultivate contentment and peace by maintaining a grateful attitude in the midst of the circumstances.

In these last days, things will often happen to cause us to become agitated. However, we must maintain our peace and free ourselves from what the Bible calls "agitating passions and moral conflicts" (2 Peter 3:1-14). Jesus experienced agitation when He knew Judas was about to betray Him (John 13:21, *Amplified Bible*), but instead of yielding to temptation, He kept His peace. We have the same power to control our emotions.

As Christians, we greatly benefit from having a worry-free life. Without worry and agitation, we can hear from God more clearly because our minds and hearts are not cluttered with negative emotions. Also, our hearts do not become weighed down by anxiety over stressful or irritating situations (Proverbs 12:25, *AMP*). When we focus on God, and remember His covenant with us, we will be encouraged. And even when we suffer for doing what is right, God promises to reward us.

What is the devil using to stir up your emotions in a negative way? Can you identify points of agitation that have infiltrated your mind and heart? If so, take those issues before the Lord. Cast your cares on Him and put yourself in remembrance of His Word, which promises peace when you keep your focus on Him. Get the Word in your mouth and make confessions of faith that eradicate negative thinking. Overcoming agitation is one decision away!

> "WE MAKE A CHOICE TO BECOME AGITATED, TROUBLED, DISTURBED, OR AFRAID, JUST LIKE WE MAKE A CHOICE TO REMAIN FOCUSED ON GOD'S WORD."

CHAPTER 24
The Victorious Power of God's Love

"And hope maketh not ashamed; because the
love of God is shed abroad in our hearts by the
Holy Ghost which is given unto us"

(Romans 5:5).

Did you know that the key to truly walking in victory and success in your life is through having a working revelation of God's love for you? I'm not just talking about knowing it in your head but *really* knowing it in your heart. Having confidence in God's love will absolutely shut down the devil's attempts to derail you with temptation, and it will enable you to do the works of Jesus without reservation. It will flush fear out of your life and keep you in a state of perpetual faith. Because of the blood of Jesus that is covering your life, God is for you and not against you—you have nothing to fear! What Jesus did put God on your side forever, and there is nothing that can separate you from His love.

Romans 8:31, 32 really communicates the reality of God's love for us. It says, "What shall we then say to these things?

If God be for us, who can be against us? He that spared not his own Son, but delivered him up for us all, how shall he not with him also freely give us all things?" We know God loves us because He did not withhold His only Son. I don't know anyone who would willingly allow his or her child to be sacrificed on behalf of someone else. I know I couldn't do it! But God's love for mankind far surpasses human love. It is this love that the Father has for us that moved Him to allow His Son to die for our sins. This love is deep and authentic, not a superficial love that is based on changing emotions. God's love never changes because He is love.

Make no mistake about it, the Father wants you to know that you are loved and valued by Him. The more you sense God's love for you, the more you'll sense good things happening in your life. The Apostle John was so confident in God's love that his enemies could not even kill him! They tried but failed and ultimately sent him to the Island of Patmos to die because there was nothing else they could do with him. He was totally immersed in the reality of God's love for him, and it sustained him even during the most difficult times of his life. He had no fear.

When you are rooted and grounded in God's love for you, it will empower you to do all things. This love is the power generator behind your faith and every other principle in the kingdom of God. You will find yourself doing the things that Jesus did with ease, such as laying hands on the sick, casting out devils, and sharing the Gospel with others, when you are driven by the love of God, and you know He loves you. This love will expel fear from your life and keep you in perfect peace, just as it did for the Apostle John.

Romans 5:5 says that the love of God has been shed abroad in our hearts by the Holy Ghost. The Holy Spirit is the Spirit of love, and that very Spirit is residing in you. Not only did He pour the love of God on the inside of you, giving you the ability to love others the way God loves them, but He has also enabled you to tap into the love God has for *you*! He wants you to know love and then go out and demonstrate that love to others.

Hope, combined with knowing God's love for you, will equal great success and victory in your life; however, you have to meditate on God's love for you on a constant basis in order to become established in it. Ephesians 3:17-19 says, "That Christ may dwell in your hearts by faith; that ye, being rooted and grounded in love, May be able to comprehend with all saints what is the breadth, and length, and depth, and height; And to know the love of Christ, which passeth knowledge, that ye might be filled with all the fullness of God." This is the will of God for your life—to believe and intimately *know* God's love for you. The more you meditate on God's love for you, the more you will experience the fullness of Him. This fullness will drive fear out of your life.

Satan has no defense against those who have a revelation of God's love for them. I encourage you to spend at least thirty minutes a day meditating on how much God loves you. He loves you so much that He will never leave you or forsake you. He will keep you and protect you, even in the midst of chaos and confusion. When the devil tries to attack your mind with fear, guilt, condemnation, or doubt, refuse to accept his thoughts. Instead, open your mouth and declare, "GOD LOVES ME!"

A LOVE THAT TRANSFORMS

God's love for us and our victories go hand in hand. When we know that God loves us, we know that He is for us, no matter what is going on in our lives. Sometimes we have been so indoctrinated with the idea that God is mad at us or is withholding something from us because of our past mistakes that it hinders our faith. Our faith works by love, which involves knowing and believing God's love for us. When we have a working revelation of this love, it will absolutely transform our lives.

We tend to focus so much of our energy on the fact that we love God that we neglect to meditate on His love for us. However, we need to spend time feeding on the truth of God's love and allowing it to sink deep into our spirits. A revelation of God's love will revolutionize your thinking. You will not be concerned with how your needs are going to be met when you know God loves you. You won't be in fear when an unexpected bill shows up in the mail. When the doctor gives you a bad report, you can take courage knowing that because of God's love for you, you are healed in Jesus' name. You can be confident that He will not withhold any good thing from you because He did not withhold His only Son (Romans 8:32).

Jesus wants to be everything to us, and it's time for us to receive Him as our everything. This means we must start confessing everything we need Him to be. What do you need Him to be in your life? If we need Him to be our healer, we have to declare it with boldness. If we need Him to be our financial prosperity, we have to say it out of our mouths. God gave Jesus to us so that He could fulfill all of our needs. He sent Jesus so that we could know and understand the maximum expression of His love for us.

The enemy will constantly try to get you to doubt God's love by bringing circumstances and situations into your life that are designed to attack your confidence. You must have faith in your heart, even when fear is knocking on the door of your mind. When different things come up that try to move you from your faith in God's love, you must say what you believe. Romans 5:5 says that the love of God has been deposited in your heart by way of the Holy Spirit. Not only does this enable you to love others with the God-kind of love, but it enables you to know God's love for you! When you really believe in this love that has been shed abroad in your heart, your hopes will not be disappointed. You will have complete confidence that God is for you and working out every situation in your life for your good.

In order to build yourself up in the revelation of God's love for you, it is imperative that you spend time meditating on the love of God every day. Find scriptures about God's love and speak them over your life. Declare that God loves you and He is unequivocally for *you*. Speak the love of God over your family and loved ones. The basis of your faith is the fact that God loves you. And if you know He loves you, then you know that whatever you expect from Him that lines up with the Word belongs to you. First John 4:9 says, "In this was manifested the love of God toward us, because that God sent his only begotten Son into the world, that we might live through him." Jesus is the ultimate love-gift, and when we have Him, we have *everything* else we will ever need or desire in this life. Our heavenly Father will make sure of that.

PRAYING IN TONGUES
ACTIVATES GOD'S LOVE

We know that perfect, or mature, love casts out fear (1 John 4:18), and since this is the case, we should be seeking ways to develop in the love of God. One of the ways we can activate the love of God in our lives is through our personal heavenly prayer language of tongues. The Believer's personal prayer language is a gift from God, and it allows you to pray in a way that directly communicates with God by way of the Holy Spirit. The love of God is in the heart of every Christian at the moment he or she receives Christ. This means that the fruit of the Spirit, which is love and its different attributes, is within the Believer, and it is activated by praying in the Holy Spirit, or praying in tongues. Jude 1:20, 21 says that

> "MAKE NO MISTAKE ABOUT IT, THE FATHER WANTS YOU TO KNOW THAT YOU ARE LOVED AND VALUED BY HIM."

when we pray in tongues we build ourselves up on our most holy faith, and we *keep* ourselves in the love of God. I cannot emphasize enough how true this is.

In my own personal life, praying in tongues has had amazing effects on my love walk. If you want to develop in the love of God, spend a significant amount of time praying in the Holy Ghost. Not only are you praying hidden wisdom and mysteries by praying in tongues, but you are stirring up the Holy Spirit inside of you. And since He is the one who is responsible for the love deposit in your recreated spirit (Romans 5:5), you are stirring up that love when you pray in your heavenly language.

The reason you are stirring up God's love in you when you pray in tongues is because praying in tongues is an operation of the Spirit of God, and anything related to God is going to be related to love. So when you pray this way, you are literally turning on the power of love within you. Not only that, but God will begin to show you ways you can demonstrate love to others. You will literally feel the love and compassion of God rising and growing within you when you spend significant time praying in tongues. In the midst of your prayers, He will give you wisdom and insight on what to do in life, especially as it relates to your relationships with others. He will also show you areas of your life where you need to exercise the love of God, and you will find yourself becoming more sensitive to times when you are *not* operating from a position of love.

As the fruit of the Spirit continues to grow in our lives, we become more conformed into the nature, character, and image of Christ. Our heavenly language of tongues has the power and ministry of the Holy Spirit, which generates, activates, and increases the fruit of the Spirit in our nature and character. This will absolutely eradicate fear in our lives because fear and love cannot coexist. Praying in tongues plays a vital role in producing the power and presence of God in your life.

God intimately cares for us. He knows the exact number of hairs that are on our heads, and He is perfecting those things that concern us. It is so important for us to believe that God loves us. This is the root to our victory as Christians. Our faith works by our knowledge of God's love for us. When we know and believe this love, we will live a fear-free life and begin to experience the supernatural power of God like never before. Believe the Love!

CHAPTER 25
Grace: The Key to Victory in Spiritual Warfare

"There is therefore now no condemnation to them which are in Christ Jesus, who walk not after the flesh, but after the Spirit" (Romans 8:1).

As Believers, we are engaged in a battle of epic proportions. The battle is between our unrenewed souls (their impulses, suggestions, and distractions) and our recreated spirits, which have been made alive with the life of God. We have an adversary, Satan, who is constantly seeking to devour us with his accusations, suggestions, and distractions. He does this by filling our minds with fear-filled thoughts. This is one of the tactics he uses to launch his attacks against us. His objective is to play on our old nature of sin, which is governed by selfishness, to move us into a place where we do not trust God but trust, instead, in our own ability to handle our situations and circumstances. We must know and understand the purpose of grace and how it is a weapon of spiritual warfare against the devil, in order to defeat him at every turn.

If you haven't noticed yet, the enemy uses specific strategies to derail Christians. He has many approaches, but one of the primary strategies he uses is getting Believers to try to gain right standing with God through their own efforts. This is all fear-based because it is founded on a lack of understanding about God's love for us, and the belief that He hasn't really completed the work that brings us into right relationship with Him. We feel as if there is something more we have to do. The devil also tells Believers that God can't really take care of us like He promises, so we have to try to take care of our needs and our situations ourselves. Everything the devil does is designed to trick us into thinking that what God does is somehow inadequate, and we need to get involved. The grace of God, however, is our weapon of spiritual warfare because it enables us to access God's rest. The devil has no defense against Believers who trust in God's grace and believe in His love for them.

When it comes to using grace to overcome the devil and his fearful suggestions, we must remember to always be strong in the Lord and His ability, not our own. Ephesians 6:10-12 says, Finally, my brethren, be strong in the Lord, and in the power of his might. Put on the whole armor of God, that ye may be able to stand against the wiles of the devil. For we wrestle not against flesh and blood, but against principalities, against powers, against the rulers of the darkness of this world, against spiritual wickedness in high places." We must understand that we do have an adversary, and we must be on guard against him. We do this by putting on our spiritual armor, which is essentially the power of God Himself. When you are wrapped in God's armor, nothing can harm you, especially the fiery darts of mental suggestions the devil tries to implant in your mind.

We cannot defeat the devil in our own ability, but God's grace working in and through our lives enables us to have the victory. The key is to realize that we are to come from a position of already being victorious, rather than trying to obtain victory. Jesus has already given us the victory through His finished work. There is nothing more for us to do except to trust, believe, and stand on the promises of God in faith.

God's grace is a supernatural empowerment from God that enables us to do *anything*. Would "anything" include defeating the enemy? Of course! With the grace of God operating in our lives, nothing is impossible. This means if the enemy tries to come against you with a bad report from the doctor in an attempt to put fear in your heart, you remind yourself of God's love for you and that you possess the ability to overcome that bad report by standing on the Word of God and staying in faith no matter what. When your finances seem to be in shambles and Satan whispers in your ear that you will never get ahead in life, boldly declare that God's grace is sufficient and that you possess the victory over lack in your life. God's grace is able to sustain you in the midst of every challenge and battle you face.

Remember that the devil can only succeed in your life if you are performance-centered or self-centered, or operating according to the Law. The Law of Moses was implemented to make people aware of their sin and point them toward their need for a Savior. The problem with the Law was that no one could keep it, even though it was righteous, holy, and good. Not only that, but the Law breeds sin consciousness, which causes condemnation. When you are trying to please God through Law-based self-effort, you will always fall short. And when you fall short, the enemy will be right there to point an accusing finger at you and beat you up with condemnation.

Because of man's inability to keep the Law, God made another covenant with man. This covenant, which secured your righteousness, was fulfilled through Jesus Christ's ultimate sacrifice on the cross of Calvary. By simply believing in what Jesus did for you, you enter into the covenant of grace, which says that no longer do you have to try to attain right-standing with God through self-effort, but you can rest in the finished work of Christ. When you have a revelation of this new covenant, as a Believer living under the dispensation of grace and not the Law, it frees you from the fear, guilt, and condemnation that come from trying to live up to a standard that can never be fulfilled. The devil cannot attack you when you are no longer operating according to legalism. Jesus fulfilled every requirement of the Law, and when you are in Him, you are free to live a fear-free life that pleases God.

We know that God has not given us a spirit of fear but a spirit of power, love, and a sound mind (2 Timothy 1:7). Having a revelation of God's grace is the key to living free from fear. When you know the grace of God is working on your behalf and that God is not mad at you, you don't have to fear anything. God's love will never be withdrawn from you, and He will finish the good work He started in you.

TOTAL DEPENDENCE ON GOD

Submitting to God is an important step in seeing victory in our lives. James 4:7 says that when we submit to God, the devil flees from us. A humble person is one who will submit to the Word of God rather than try

> "WE CANNOT DEFEAT THE DEVIL IN OUR OWN ABILITY, BUT GOD'S GRACE WORKING IN AND THROUGH OUR LIVES ENABLES US TO HAVE THE VICTORY."

to do things his or her own way. God gives grace to the humble, but He resists the proud person (1 Peter 5:5-8; Luke 18:10-15). The devil seeks to devour the proud person who is focused on self-effort, but not every Christian is devourable. God's grace will put the odds in your favor in the midst of spiritual warfare when you humble yourself and submit to His way.

It is usually in the midst of spiritual warfare that we are tempted to do things our own way. Our emotions, physical senses, and prior ways of handling things often try to speak to us loud and clear. If we give attention to anything and any voice other than the voice of the Holy Spirit and the voice of God's Word, we can easily slip over into pride and self-effort when the pressure is on. We must make a quality decision to rely on God's Word and make it our final authority, no matter what it looks like. When we submit ourselves to Him, He will equip us with more and more grace. We must not allow the enemy to cause us to become fearful, condemned, or distracted during this critical time.

Again, we have to constantly put ourselves in remembrance of the fact that we are to draw our strength from God in the midst of the battle. We are to put on His Word and establish ourselves in our new identity in Christ (Ephesians 6:11, *AMP*). We don't wrestle against human beings but against the powers of darkness. In a practical setting, this means that if the enemy is trying to come against us through a person, we must resist engaging with that person or operating in our flesh. Instead, we are to handle the attack God's way, which is how we submit to Him. We can respond to difficult people by binding the enemy operating through them, praying for them, and continuing to walk in love. This is one way we can humble ourselves under God's hand when we are being spiritually attacked by others. You will find that the more you choose God's way of dealing with these types of situations, the more readily the enemy will get out of your way.

When we are facing spiritual battles, we must remind ourselves to cast our cares and burdens on the Lord because He cares for us. When we worry, it is an indication that we don't truly trust God. Satan's "roar" is designed to put fear and terror in us, but those who come out on top are the ones who are submitted to God's grace. Satan will try to impersonate God and make us feel as if God is angry with us. He will throw every sin and mistake in our faces to make us think that we did something to deserve what we are going through. This only fuels the cycle of self-effort! We try to "do" something to get on God's good side rather than believe His love will never fail us and that nothing we do can qualify or disqualify us from His goodness toward us. God has made a covenant with us as New Testament Believers to never pour down His wrath upon us (Isaiah 54:9). Take heart in knowing that He has given us ultimate favor because of our relationship with His Son.

KNOWING WHO YOU ARE

Knowing your identity in Christ is so vital to accessing the grace of God by faith. As a born-again Christian, your spirit has been recreated and the old things have passed away (2 Corinthians 5:17, 18). As a Believer, you now possess the nature of Christ, which includes the grace of God. That grace has been deposited in your spirit! When you are in Him, you are in grace. Now all you have to do is withdraw that power by faith. You do this by meditating on the grace of God and declaring His Word. Your faith in the grace is released when you confess and declare that the grace of God is operating in your life.

Satan's primary job is to make us feel as if we are not worthy of God's precious gifts. He tries to condemn us when we do something wrong, and he uses the law to strengthen our temptation to sin. He wants us to believe that God is withholding His goodness from us. However, the Bible is one continual account of God's goodness and love toward His people. He is gracious and generous and will continue to be this way because His nature is love! He freely gives good gifts to His children, and grace is one of those gifts. It is so exciting to know that God has not left us alone to fight life's battles on our own. When we become new creatures in Christ, we are infused with the power of God on every level. We must have confidence in who we are in Him in order to win.

God is for us, and we can place our complete trust in Him because He has given us right standing with Himself through Jesus Christ. We no longer have to feel condemned or guilty over our sins now that we are in Christ (Romans 8:1). We can walk boldly through life, knowing that fear can never dominate us when we are under grace. Nothing the devil does can stop us because we hold the keys to victory. God's grace is sufficient to keep us, sustain us, and give us the advantage in life. All we have to do is receive it by faith and develop our confidence in it. In doing so, we will find ourselves walking in a level of absolute mastery over the devil and winning every spiritual battle in life.